Dating WITH ❧ INTEGRITY ❧

Dating WITH INTEGRITY

Honoring Christ In Your Relationships With The Opposite Sex

JOHN HOLZMANN

Wolgemuth & Hyatt, Publishers, Inc.
Brentwood, Tennessee

The mission of Wolgemuth & Hyatt, Publishers, Inc. is to publish and distribute books that lead individuals toward:

- A personal faith in the one true God: Father, Son, and Holy Spirit;

- A lifestyle of practical discipleship; and

- A worldview that is consistent with the historic, Christian faith.

Moreover, the Company endeavors to accomplish this mission at a reasonable profit and in a manner which glorifies God and serves His Kingdom.

Wolgemuth & Hyatt, Publishers, Inc.
1749 Mallory Lane, Suite 110
Brentwood, Tennessee 37027

Library of Congress Cataloging-in-Publication Data

Holzmann, John
    Dating with integrity : honoring Christ in your relationships with
the opposite sex / John Holzmann.
        p. cm.
    ISBN 1-56121-022-6
    1. Dating (Social customs)—Religious aspects—Christianity.
    2. Love. 3. Sex—Religious aspects—Christianity. I. Title.
HQ801.H73 1990
646.7'7—dc20   90-38783
                                                                  CIP

To Sarita, Sunbeam,
the wife of my youth

CONTENTS

ACKNOWLEDGMENTS

F ew books there must be that are solo efforts! From formulating one's ideas, to researching the contents, to putting one's conclusions into words, and then polishing the manuscript until it shines: an author needs friends. And editors. And before a manuscript becomes a book, one also needs graphic artists, designers, typesetters, and printers. Not to mention a publisher who is willing to risk his capital. How well I know!

To those who gave me special encouragement—to my mother and father who raised me to believe and think as I do and taught me to value myself; to my brother David and my sister Miriam; to the Higbys (especially Doug), and to Kevin, Robbie and all the others at the U.S. Center for World Mission who tried to apply what I was saying and gave me feedback; to Elisabeth Elliot who wrote me two notes she may not even remember; to Kerry Lovering of SIM (formerly Sudan Interior Mission) who gave me similar advice to Ms. Elliot's and showed me how to put it into practice; to Dan Van't Kerkhoff of Baker Book House who went three rounds with me only to watch me sell the manuscript to another publisher; and to Sarita who, though she didn't believe it would ever be published, was willing to let me work on the manuscript anyway: to you, special thanks. But thank you to all the others, too—the hundreds—who helped make *Dating with Integrity* become what it is. I couldn't have done it without you.

And, Lord Jesus, thank *You* for making it all possible.

Keep on loving each other as brothers.

Hebrews 13:1

Make every effort to add to your . . . godliness, brotherly kindness; and to brotherly kindness, love.

2 Peter 1:5–7

INTRODUCTION

W hen Steve and I originally agreed to meet at Landon Hall, an all-girl dorm at Michigan State, it was with the idea that we would meet once a week for private conversation. No one knew us at Landon so we figured we'd be undisturbed. That didn't last long, however. Soon we discovered so many other advantages to eating at Landon Hall that our once-a-week interludes became a daily habit.

Our dorms were on the western edge of the campus, a mile from the nearest classroom building. No matter where our classes were held before lunch, Landon was closer.

Landon was also cozier. The cafeterias in our dorms served two to three thousand students each meal; Landon served fewer than four hundred.

Our dorms were a clash and glare of steel, concrete, fluorescent lights, and huge picture windows. Landon was filled with the quiet elegance of rich wood paneling, thick carpets, and drapes. The food, too, though very good in our dorms, was just a bit better in Landon.

Finally, we'd struck up a relationship with a pretty and intelligent Christian girl named Sarita.

But then one day a few weeks after we first met Sarita, I realized Steve and I weren't accomplishing what we'd originally come to Landon to do. Our "private conversation" had become a threesome, then four, . . . five, . . . six, . . . a group of almost twenty Christian students who regularly ate lunch together at Landon Hall. Steve and I were never eating alone anymore.

I suggested to Steve that maybe it was time we pursued the purposes for which we'd originally come. That afternoon we walked past the table where all our new friends were and sat down to eat by ourselves.

About twenty minutes later, having finished my first helping, I went to get seconds. As I walked by, Sarita looked at me and I nodded. "Hey, John," she responded, "why don't you guys sit with us anymore?"

Anymore? I thought to myself. But I told her why Steve and I had come to Landon in the first place and explained that we'd simply decided it was time to pursue our original purpose.

"Oh." She looked disappointed but let me go on.

As I proceeded to the serving line, my mind was in turmoil. I wondered how I should respond. Something about that word *anymore*, something in the way she'd said it, something in the way she'd responded to me at other times, too. I had no doubts Sarita wanted to be my girlfriend. The problem was, I didn't want to be her boyfriend . . . or anyone else's boyfriend, for that matter. I knew we needed to talk.

By the time Steve and I finished eating, the cafeteria was almost empty. I noticed Sarita and the person she had been talking to were just getting up to leave.

Steve and I parted and I walked over to Sarita, my heart pounding within my chest. "Got a few minutes?" I asked.

"Sure," she said. She could tell something was bothering me.

She sat back down. I eased myself into the chair opposite her and hesitated a moment before launching in.

"This afternoon you asked, 'Why don't you guys sit with us *anymore?*'" I said. "Do you realize, today is the first time in three weeks we haven't sat with you? That hardly establishes a trend."

She looked at me quizzically, not sure if she understood what I was driving at but recognizing a hint of accusation in what I'd said.

I mentioned some other things she'd done that made it clear to me she wanted to be my girlfriend: listening more intensely when I spoke, smiling winsomely whenever she caught my eye.

"I want you to know," I said, "I'm not interested in being your boyfriend. I'm not interested in being anyone's boyfriend. I'm your brother, your brother in the Lord. I'd like you to treat me like your brother, and I want to treat you like my sister. If there's something I'd do with, to, or for one of my natural-born sisters, then I'm willing to do it with, to, or for you. If there's something I wouldn't do in their case, then I won't do it in yours, either. I'd appreciate it if you would treat me the same way."

Sarita was stunned—partially by my audacity in broaching the topic and partially by the strangeness of my ideas. She'd never met a guy before who'd objected to entering into a boy-friend-girlfriend relationship. And to have him talk of treating her like a sister was totally outside her experience.

Despite Sarita's inexperience with the idea, the commitment I made to her that day was no different from the commitment I was making to every woman I knew. I had become convinced that I needed to treat all my sisters in Christ as if they were my sisters in the flesh. Over the years I found not only that this commitment was right, but that it could help me distinguish Biblically appropriate behavior from behavior that was inappropriate. It could help me distinguish friendly, upbuilding behavior from behavior that tends to stifle and destroy relationships. Ultimately, it could help me avoid some of the most treacherous ambushes Satan has ever devised for destroying God's people.

When Sarita and I became engaged almost a year after we first met, we felt we knew each other better than we had ever known any other friends. I am convinced that behaving as a brother toward all the rest of my sisters gave me similar privileges with them: it enabled me to get to know them better, too—better than almost any of their boyfriends ever knew them.

☙ ☙ ☙

By the time I was fourteen or fifteen, I'm sure I'd heard of the idea of Christians being each other's brothers and sisters. In the church where I spent my later elementary and junior high school years, people spoke of "brothers and sisters in Christ." I'm sure I also ran across those words in my normal reading of Scripture. But to this day I can't remember having ever heard any teaching on the subject of treating brothers and sisters in Christ as if they were brothers and sisters in the flesh.

Having never been taught this idea, therefore, and having never known anyone who actually attempted to put it into practice, when I was fifteen I blithely followed the pattern my culture placed before me: I entered my first boyfriend-girlfriend relationship.

Carrie and I first met sometime late in the fall of our sophomore year in high school. We talked together and soon found we enjoyed each other's company. As much as any high school sophomores can spend time together, we did: between classes, at lunch, on Saturdays, and at church. We were friends.

And then one night our relationship changed. We had gone to a Campus Life meeting held in a farmhouse at the top of a hill. The meeting broke up late.

My mother was waiting to drive us home. She was parked on the street at the bottom of the hill. The driveway meandered a long way around before it reached the street, so Carrie and I decided to take the shortcut—straight down the hill.

Rocks and weeds dotted our path, it was dark out, and I didn't want Carrie to fall, so I reached out and grabbed her hand as we began our descent. It was the first time I'd touched her—first time I'd touched any girl in that way, for that matter—but she didn't seem to mind. It was a friendly thing to do.

And then it happened. We reached the bottom of the hill, began to walk, and neither one of us let go! Suddenly I realized something I had not been sure about before: Carrie liked me. No, she loved me. She *loved* me! I was loved! I was *in* love. Carrie and I were no longer friends. Suddenly, we were boyfriend and girlfriend.

Oh! the feelings I had as my mom drove us home that night! Carrie and I had launched out into the shining sea of boyfriend-girlfriend relationships. It was the beginning of something glorious, a great adventure. . . .

It lasted nine months. And then it was over. Unexpectedly, with shell-shocked devastation, I heard Carrie say, "I want to break up with you. I can't take it anymore."

I was far too possessive of her, she said. My affection was too confining. She needed more freedom. The result was, Carrie and I were "through" and our "endless love" had led to something other than lifelong wedded bliss.

I spent many late nights after our breakup thinking and praying about what had gone wrong between us. I tried to figure out how I could change things, what I could have done differently, what I could yet do in order to win her back. It took several months before I came to rest about the whole situation.

About a year after Carrie and I broke up, I started going with Kirsten. Our relationship began much the same way Carrie's and mine had. One night after attending a movie with a couple of friends, Kirsten and I were sitting in the back seat of the car. I had this feeling. I wanted to hold her hand. I reached out—it seemed the right thing to do—and took her hand in mine. She clasped mine in return.

Oh, the joy! Once more I enjoyed that delicious, warm feeling of acceptance. Kirsten and I were boyfriend and girlfriend.

Over the course of the next seven months or so, our ability to communicate was corroded by an overstimulated physical relationship and, soon after graduation, we broke up. The end for Kirsten and me was not quite as traumatic as when Carrie and I broke up, but I knew it had not been as simple as if we had been mere friends.

I began to look around at the relationships my friends were involved in and soon discovered that my experiences were not unusual. The pain of breaking up was common to most boyfriend-girlfriend relationships: at least one of the members felt undone; someone almost always felt betrayed.

When his girlfriend broke up with him, one of the guys at my high school bawled his eyes out in the middle of the school hallway; you could hear him crying from twenty yards away. Another girl I knew was virtually paralyzed with grief for five weeks after her "one-and-only" broke up with her. She spent most of her time lying in bed, reading old love letters, and crying uncontrollably. She could hardly bring herself to eat, she was so devastated! Some threatened suicide when told their loved ones wanted to leave. Others simply bore their pain in silence.

However it occurred, I knew that breaking up was hard to do!

But why? I asked myself. Why all the joy and happiness at the beginning of a boyfriend-girlfriend relationship and why all the pain and agony at the end? What's so hard about breaking up?

I determined never to enter a boyfriend-girlfriend relationship again until I'd found the answer. I didn't want to hurt another person by finding myself breaking up with her.

Why is Breaking Up So Hard to Do?

By the time I entered college, I thought I had a pretty good idea of how to avoid boyfriend-girlfriend relationships—simply *avoid holding hands!* That had been the way my relationships with Carrie and Kirsten had begun: I had held their hands. I figured that's the way it must be in all boyfriend-girlfriend relationships.

Despite my naiveté in this matter, my insight, such as it was, helped me avoid becoming someone's boyfriend before I was ready.

Still—or, rather, with greater urgency, now that I'd committed myself not to go with someone until I'd found the answer—the question bothered me: *Why is breaking up so painful?*

As I was thinking about this question one day, it dawned on me: boyfriend-girlfriend and marriage relationships have a number of characteristics in common:

- *Both involve ownership.* When people in these relationships say, "I'm yours, you're mine!" they mean a lot more than merely, "I'm in relationship with you and you're in relationship with me." Among other things, they mean they have given each other at least a limited right to determine what each of them will do, and how, when, and with whom they will do it.

- *Both are mutual relationships.* It doesn't work to have one person thinking of the other as boyfriend or girlfriend while the second person thinks of the first as merely a friend or acquaintance. So, too, in marriage: you're either both married or you're not.

- *Both are exclusive relationships.* Not only are they unique relationships—you have only one boyfriend, girlfriend, husband, or wife at a time—but they are relationships in which the partners allow no rivals. There is no such thing as a "best" boyfriend or girlfriend, "best" serious dating partner, or "best" husband or wife (each of these being compared to a "regular" version).

- *Both include physical-sexual intimacy.* In Christian circles, of course, we are taught that people who aren't married aren't supposed to "go all the way;" but sexually oriented hand-holding, hugging, and kissing (see chapter 7) are considered proper. Indeed, participants in boyfriend-girlfriend and marriage relationships sense that something is wrong if they cannot engage in some form of physical intimacy. Such intimacy is not only expected, it is demanded as a *right*.

- *Participants in both relationships sense they have some kind of obligation to keep going together.* Even when one person's positive regard for or interest in the other person has disappeared, he or she will often feel obligated not to terminate the relationship. Whatever good reasons there may be for these relationships to end, they tend to drag on anyway. When a person finally decides to make a break, she will still tend to agonize over how best to state her case. What should she say? What's her justification? Without grave, mitigating circumstances, it is considered inappropriate and dishonorable to terminate one of these relationships. Staying together is certainly perceived as honorable, while breaking up is not.

- Unless one of the partners dies, *both relationships require some form of spoken end.* Participants in such relationships can never merely drift apart or drift into another form of relationship. Even if one partner physically walks out on the other, the relationship isn't automatically dissolved. Something has to be said. In marriage, a legal declaration, a divorce decree, has to be issued. In boyfriend-girlfriend relationships, if one person walks out on the other, until something is stated in words, it's not clear if the relationship has been terminated or if the participants have merely had a bad argument. And so something is always said when these relationships come to an end.

- *Change in both relationships occurs suddenly, noticeably, and, except in extreme circumstances, with the knowledge of both partners.* A long period of growing affection or disaffection may precede the decisive moment, but when a couple first start going together or when they marry—as also when they break up or divorce—they will have few questions in the future about where or when these events took place. Ask people who have been involved in boyfriend-girlfriend relationships when they began going together or when they broke up and they can always give you an answer. If they can't tell you exact dates and times, they can always tell you where it happened and the circumstances that led up to the change.

As I thought about these similarities, it hit me: I know why all these things are true for married couples. Marriage partners have been through a wedding. They have made *vows* to one another. It is because of their vows "to take . . . to have and to hold" that married couples feel the responsibilities of ownership and mutuality. It is the marriage vow "to cling to him (her) only" that makes the relationship exclusive. The part of the vows that speaks of "as long as we both shall live" creates the sense of obligation to *keep going* even after the relationship has become hurtful. . . .

But what about boyfriends and girlfriends? Could their relationships be based on vows, too? As you'll see in chapter 4, this is the very conclusion to which I finally came.

I didn't want to come to this conclusion; it was something I was forced to do against my will. Again as you'll read in chapter 4, it forever precluded me from becoming involved in boyfriend-girlfriend relationships. Instead, I found I was obliged to pursue brother-sister relationships. Not only so, but, as I obeyed God in this area, I discovered that brother-sister relationships were far more than an obligation; they were a great privilege. More than any of my friends who followed our culturally-approved boyfriend-girlfriend and "serious" dating patterns, I found I was able to bless the people around me. I was able to show more effective concern for a greater number of my brothers and sisters. I was able to be more honest, to communicate more effectively, and to avoid those unwanted but very real feelings of mutual obligation men and women often encounter in dating relationships. I found myself free from all the snares with which people entrap themselves when they become involved in physical-sexual intimacy before they have made a marriage commitment: the snare of the self-centered and physical focus that tends to rot the heart out of so many dating relationships; the feelings of betrayal when a couple reneges on the promises they have unintentionally conveyed to one another through their sexual intimacy. Even more than all these things, I found I was free to spend time with my sisters: lots of time, different kinds of time, time in which we lived reality and redeemed the time. Brother-sister relationships, I discovered, are truly a gracious gift from a loving God.

ᕽ ᕽ ᕽ

The purpose of this book is threefold:

1. *To present Biblical arguments* for why you should treat members of the opposite sex as brothers and sisters rather than boyfriends, girlfriends, or "serious" dating partners.

2. *To develop a workable model* of brother-sister relationships.

3. *To give solid advice* about making brother-sister relationships work.

I speak of brother-sister dating as dating with *integrity* because integrity means completeness, wholeness, soundness . . . as well as honesty and sincerity. I am convinced that when a man and woman treat each other as I suggest here—as brother and sister—their relationship will be marked by completeness, wholeness, soundness, honesty, and sincerity.

I have written as I have in order to convince you of the truth of what I say. My goal, however, is not to force you into my mold. I do not want to do your thinking for you. I want to do whatever I can to help you think through the issues for yourself.

I speak of trying to develop a workable *model* of brother-sister relationships because that is all I feel I can do. Since so little has been written on the subject, my fondest dream is merely that you will wrestle with the concepts and issues I present and then come to your own conclusions. I expect that you will disagree with me on at least one or two points. The big question has to do with the over-all model: Is it workable? Is it something God wants you to emulate? Is it something that will bless you and that will enable you more fully to bless the people around you?

As long as you are honest with the facts, your heart is set on pleasing God, and you commit yourself to do whatever He tells you, I am confident He will lead you into all truth (see John 16:13). What Jesus said concerning His own teaching is true here as well: "If anyone chooses to do God's will, he will find out whether my teaching comes from God or whether I speak on my own" (John 7:17).

If what I say is, indeed, from God, then you can be sure it will free you—free you in ways, perhaps, you weren't even aware you needed to be freed. As Jesus said, "If you hold to my teaching, . . . then you will know the truth, and the truth will set you free" (John 8:31–32). I found freedom in treating my sisters in Christ as I would my biological sisters; I am confident that if you follow a similar pattern, you will find freedom, too.

I will give you principles. I will help define and differentiate. Ultimately, however, you will have to apply what you read in these pages to your experiences in daily life. That's why I've concluded most chapters with special "Questions for Study and Discussion." "Is it true?" "Why or why not?" "If it is true, what will I do about it?" These are questions for you to answer.

My desire is that by the end of this book you will know what you believe about these things and then act upon your convictions.

John Holzmann
Pasadena, California
17 May 1990

Questions for Study and Discussion

1. In your opinion, what distinguishes boyfriend-girlfriend relationships from regular friendships or brother-sister relationships?

    a. Compare and contrast the way boyfriends and girlfriends treat each other with the way regular friends and brothers and sisters treat one another.

    b. Compare and contrast the attitudes participants in these various relationships have toward each other, toward their relationships, and toward outsiders.

    c. Compare and contrast the way these relationships begin and end.

    What makes a couple change from being "just friends" to being boyfriend and girlfriend?

    In what ways are these relationships the same and in what ways different?

2. What do you think of the idea of treating members of the opposite sex as you would your own brother or sister? Have you had any experience with it? Does it make sense? Is it workable? Why or why not?

3. If you could have a "dream" date, what would it include?

4. Imagine you are married. You are in your current financial and living situation, but every night instead of going home to the place you now live, you go home to your husband or wife. *How would you get to know your husband or wife better than you know him or her already?* Would you go out to eat? Go to a movie? Sit home and watch TV? Read the paper? Hug, kiss, and pet? Talk? What would you do? Where would you do it? And *why?* Write down your thoughts.

5. Now imagine you're not married. You're yourself: you live where you live, you work where you work, you go to school where you go to school. Everything is the way it really is. In that context, how do you try to get to know— really *know*—members of the opposite sex? Write down your answer.

6. Compare your answers in 4 and 5, above. Are there differences? Why or why not?

7. What friendship relationships (same sex or opposite) have you had that would make good models for a brother-sister relationship?

   a. What made those friendships special to you?

   b. What activities did you do together?

   c. Is there anything about those friendships you would not want to make a part of a brother-sister relationship? Why or why not?

8. Answer the same questions for any boyfriend-girlfriend relationships you've been in. Have you had any that would make good models for a brother-sister relationship?

   a. What made those boyfriend-girlfriend relationships special to you?

   b. What activities did you and your boyfriend or girlfriend do together?

c. Is there anything about those boyfriend-girlfriend relationships that you would not want to make a part of a
brother-sister relationship? Why or why not?

9. Make a list of all the things you might do with a regular
friend that would make a good date with a member of the
opposite sex. (A few ideas have been provided to get you
thinking.)

a. Ride bikes.

b. Shop.

c. Bake cookies.

d. Go out to eat (something light and fairly inexpensive).

e. Pray.

f.

g.

h.

i.

(Continue your list on a separate sheet of paper. Put together at least fifteen ideas.)

PART ONE

PRINCIPLES

Make my joy complete by being like-minded, having the same love, being one in spirit and purpose. Do nothing out of selfish ambition or vain conceit, but in humility consider others better than yourselves. Each of you should look not only to your own interests, but also to the interests of others. Your attitude should be the same as that of Christ Jesus.

Philippians 2:2–5

Each one should use whatever gift he has received to serve others . . . so that in all things God may be praised through Jesus Christ.

1 Peter 4:10–11

1

WHAT DO YOU HAVE IN MIND?

Brothers and Sisters Remember Their Purpose: To Bless

T wo members of a basketball team were standing on the sidelines during the middle of practice arguing about the meaning of *out-of-bounds*. "Coach," one of them asked, "does your foot have to be all the way over the line to be out-of-bounds?"

"Yeah," said his teammate. "What if you just step on the line? Or what if you just touch it?"

The players were shocked when the coach exploded: "Gentlemen! You know something? I really don't give a rip what *out-of-bounds* means right now!

"We're in the middle of practice and I've asked you to shoot baskets! Do you realize we're ten weeks into the season, and neither one of you has made a single point? You're over there on the sidelines nit-picking over what *out-of-bounds* means while our competition is eating us alive on the boards! Forget what *out-of-bounds* means and *concentrate on the goal*. We're not here to push people out of bounds; we're here to make baskets!"

As they drifted over to the free-throw line, one of the players muttered to the other, "What's eating him? It was just a simple question."

Too often we're like those basketball players. We're asking the right questions at the wrong time.

Asking the Right Questions at the Wrong Time

Many Christian singles are so overwhelmed by the problems they're having in their boyfriend-girlfriend relationships, they never stop to ask why it is they got involved in the relationships in the first place: What were they trying to achieve when they first started going together? And what are they trying to achieve now?

A girl wrote to a columnist at a leading Christian youth magazine:

> I'm thirteen years old and the farthest I've ever gone with a guy is kissing. Never exploring. I know some guys want to do more, and if they tried I don't know that I could say no if I liked them a lot. But I don't want to do anything like that until I'm married.
>
> Just a while ago, I met a guy at a Christian conference in Iowa. A few days later we made out and he started to go up my shirt, but stopped. I was really relieved. I'm a Christian and have been since I was seven. But I don't always show it, even though I want to show it. What should I do about the exploring? How do you stop a guy before it's too late, without getting him mad?

The columnist responded,

> Your letter has posed . . . one of the major dilemmas young people face in their dating relationships. . . .
>
> I think you're absolutely right in wanting to wait for marriage. One of the best ways to make sure you will is to set your limits early in a relationship. As soon as a guy begins to explore, or anytime you feel him beginning to unbutton or unhook something, stop everything and say, "Hey, what do you have in

mind?" That kind of conversation ought to slow him down. If it doesn't, you know where you stand.

Don't give in. After all, if a guy really loves you, he will respect your wishes. Love doesn't force itself on someone else. Love never seeks to make the other person uncomfortable. Love doesn't make the person do something he or she doesn't want to do.

So draw the line. And hold it. Ten years from now you'll be glad you did.[1]

I thought the columnist's response was absurd. It wasn't that I disagreed with him about "draw[ing] the line and hold[ing] it." I am in full accord that if you wait to have sex until you're married, "you'll be glad you did."

What bothered me was that he implied the girl should expect guys to feel up her body. "Sooner or later you're going to be faced with this situation, so you'd better plan for it," he seemed to say. "So as soon as a guy begins to explore, or any time you feel him beginning to unbutton or unhook something, stop everything. . . ."

It seems to me, a woman—a Christian woman, anyway, a Christian woman out on a date with a self-proclaimed Christian guy—needs a plan for *if* such a thing should happen. Not *when*, *as soon as*, or *any time* it happens!

But the columnist's expectations about what should happen in a dating relationship were only the tip of the iceberg. There was something far more insidious about his reply.

Taking Account of One's Purpose

Imagine a "Dear Abby" offering sympathy to a reader who has been driving thirty miles per hour on an interstate highway. The reader feels abused by other motorists who honk at her, yell out the window, and shake their fists as they drive by.

The columnist responds:

Dear Abused,
Your letter poses one of the major dilemmas every driver faces on the interstate highway system.

I think you're absolutely right in wanting to drive at a speed that's comfortable for you. One of the best ways to make sure you will is to set your cruise control when you first get on the highway. As soon as someone begins to honk at you or anytime they make an angry gesture in your direction, motion for them to pull to the side of the road. When they've stopped, ask, "Hey, what do you have in mind?" That ought to slow them down.

Of course, no columnist would dare to write such horrible advice. Driving thirty miles per hour on an interstate is no dilemma, and motorists who want to go faster than thirty are under no obligation to answer a stupid question about what they have in mind! "Abused" doesn't need counsel in how to respond to motorists who are irate at her thirty-mile-per-hour obstruction of the interstate highway system. She needs to be told to *get off the road.* Interstate highways weren't designed for scenic tours; they were designed for high-speed travel.

The columnist in *Campus Life* urged the young woman to ask her boyfriends what they have in mind whenever they start to undress her. He would have served her better if he had told her to consider more seriously what she has in mind in establishing relationships with guys in the first place. Why, for instance, does she think it's okay to "make out" with her boyfriend? What is she trying to accomplish in pursuing such relationships with young men? Before asking her boyfriend what he wants, this girl needs to ask herself what she has in mind in going out with him.

You see, God has a higher purpose for us and a higher purpose for our relationships with members of the opposite sex than merely giving us kicks or providing thrills for our friends.

Blessed to Be a Blessing

Throughout the Scriptures, God makes it clear He wants us to *bless* our neighbors, our brothers and sisters. God hasn't told us to do whatever we can to seek a blessing for ourselves. Instead, He says, "*I* will bless you" (Genesis 12:2–3; 22:17; 26:3; Deuteronomy 7:12ff; Hebrews 6:13–20). From the very beginning of the Bible,

God teaches us that we are to trust *Him* to bless us; *we* are to bless others (see Genesis 12:3; 18:18–19; Matthew 16:25; Luke 6:28). There are many places in Scripture where this truth is evident, but I would like to call your attention especially to one.

Leviticus 19:18 tells us, "Love your neighbor as yourself." According to Jesus, this command is the second greatest commandment (see Matthew 22:39). It is also the basis for the Golden Rule: "In everything, do to others what you would have them do to you" (Matthew 7:12).

How far are we supposed to go in seeking to bless the people around us? Jesus says we need to go as far as losing our lives— and not only for our friends, but for our enemies as well (see Matthew 10:39; John 12:24–26; Matthew 5:44; Romans 12:9–21). And how are we to love these people and lose our lives for them? By serving them, by loving them as Jesus loved us, by considering them better than ourselves (see John 13:13–15; Galatians 5:13; John 13:34–35; Ephesians 5:1–2; Philippians 2:3–4). "This is how we know what love is: Jesus Christ laid down his life for us. And we ought to lay down our lives for our brothers" (1 John 3:16).

According to God, our purpose in life, the reason He made and redeemed us, is to bless our neighbors by serving Him, giving honor to His name, and thus introducing our neighbors to our Father and teaching them to obey everything He has commanded (see Matthew 5:13–16; 28:18–20; Ephesians 1:11–14; 1 Peter 2:9). Ultimately, our purpose is to praise God by helping to "bring all things in heaven and on earth together under one head, even Christ" (Ephesians 1:10; see also Genesis 18:18–19; 1 Corinthians 15:23–28; Colossians 1:10–14).

How strange and awesome these ideas sound when compared with the questions I hear many people ask about their relationships with members of the opposite sex!

- "My boyfriend is beating me. What should I do?"

- "How far is too far?"

- "My boyfriend is really possessive. If I even want to go out with my girlfriends, he makes a big scene."

- "I know it's wrong to have sex before marriage, but my girlfriend and I really love each other."

- "Three weeks ago my girlfriend broke up with me. Now she says she thinks it was a mistake."

- "I'm not ugly, but I'm not good-looking either. It seems all the men are interested in women with nice figures. How do I get a man to value me as a person?"

These are all good questions. They are valid concerns. But does God want these to be our primary questions and concerns? Or are they like the questions the thirteen-year old girl and the two basketball players were asking?

Yes, young woman. You need to set limits and be able to tell a guy no. But what are you doing "making out" with him in the first place? What are you trying to say to him? *Why* are you trying to say it? *What do you have in mind?*

Yes, gentlemen. The definition of *out-of-bounds* is related to the game of basketball. But what difference does it make how *out-of-bounds* is defined if you can't make baskets? Are you here to play basketball or *tae kwon do*? *What do you have in mind?*

To all the questions sincere and serious daters ask, there are answers, answers they ought to know. But somehow I have the impression that in most cases there are more important questions these people ought to be asking or ought to have asked a long time ago.

Measuring Success

It doesn't matter where you draw the line for sexual intimacy if you've forgotten your primary purpose: to bless the world and help lead your friends to a more intimate and fruitful relationship with Christ. It makes no difference if you are able to have fun in your relationships if that "fun" entails compromising your integrity.

Dating relationships are not successful merely because you and your friends have enjoyed yourselves and remained free from pregnancy, abortion, sexually transmitted diseases, and the pain of breaking up. You won't achieve God's purposes simply by avoiding stifling possessiveness, by refusing to "lead someone on," or by failing to imply vows you don't mean to fulfill.

Yes, sexual intercourse outside of marriage, stifling possessiveness, physical and mental abuse, "leading another person on"—all these things should be avoided. But God wants you to judge your relationships by higher standards than these. He's not merely interested in what things you'll *avoid,* but in what things you'll *do*: how well you'll bless your brothers and sisters; how well you'll lead them to faith and obedience; how upright your speech will be; how loving your actions.

On the lowest level you need to ask yourself: Do I want to get to know members of the opposite sex? Do I want to get to know them *well?*

And having come to know them, how well do I want to bless them? Some people figure they've done enough when they learn how to push another person's emotional and physical buttons and give them temporary thrills. Will I settle for that? Or am I committed to blessing them with all the blessings with which Christ has blessed me? Will I be content to limit my contacts with members of the opposite sex, seeking only to bless one member at a time? Or will I seek to bless as many brothers and sisters as I possibly can and give them the blessings of God—the very best blessings with which I could possibly bless them?

Ultimately, there's only one question we have to answer when it comes to our relationships with other people: What am I after? What do I have in mind? Are my goals the goals God has in mind for me? Or are they goals I've established for myself?

"Do nothing out of selfish ambition or vain conceit, but in humility consider others better than yourselves," Paul says in Philippians 2:3–8. "Each of you should look not only to your own interests, but also to the interests of others."

"You . . . were called to be free . . . [in order to] serve one another in love," says Galatians 5:13. Christ died for you so that you "should no longer live for [yourself] but for him who died for [you]" (2 Corinthians 5:15).

In 1 Peter 4:10–11, we are told, "Each one should use whatever gift he has received to serve others . . . so that in all things God may be praised through Jesus Christ."

Brothers and sisters remember—they are required to remember—what it is God wants them to do. Brothers and sisters remember their purpose: to bless the people around them.

Questions for Study and Discussion

1. Have you remembered God's purpose for you in your relationships with members of the opposite sex? If so, what evidence can you give to prove it?

   a. How have you blessed the people you've been dating?

   b. How have you and the people you've been dating blessed others?

2. According to the following passages, how can you bless the people around you? List all the ways God wants to use you in your relationships with other people. Also record any attitudes He wants you to exhibit toward others.

   a. Matthew 5–7

   b. Romans 12:4–21; 14:15–19; 15:1–2, 5–7

   c. 1 Corinthians 6:18–20

   d. 1 Corinthians 12–13

   e. 2 Corinthians 5:15

   f. Galatians 5:13–23

   g. Ephesians 1:4–14

   h. Ephesians 4:1–6:18

   i. Philippians 2:3–8

   j. James 3:13–18

k. 1 Peter 2:17; 3:8–11; 4:7–11

l. 1 John 3:16–18

3. According to Luke 10:25–37, who are you required to bless? Who is the "neighbor" you are required to love in the same manner that you love yourself?

4. What specific steps do you plan to take within the next week to bless your dating partners and the other people around you?

A new commandment I give you: Love one another. As I have loved you, so you must love one another. All men will know that you are my disciples if you love one another.

John 13:34–35

If anyone says, "I love God," yet hates his brother, he is a liar. For anyone who does not love his brother, whom he has seen, cannot love God, whom he has not seen. And he has given us this command: Whoever loves God must also love his brother.

1 John 4:20–21

2

LOVING AS JESUS LOVED

Brothers and Sisters Treat All Members of the Body with Equal Concern

I was in college. It was about eight o'clock one cold, drizzly night when the phone rang. A friend of mine, Garry, was on the line.

"Hey, John!" he said. "You think you can drive me down to Meijer's to pick up a few boards for shelves in my room?"

"You want to go right now?" I asked, hoping he would say no.

"I'd like to," he said.

"Yeah. Well. Okay." I sounded as unenthusiastic as possible.

When I got to his house about ten blocks away, I stopped, tapped the horn a couple of times, and waited. It began to rain. Garry didn't come.

I looked out of my window impatiently. *What is this?* I thought. *He calls me up and makes me come all the way over here, and he isn't even ready for me!*

A minute passed. I hit the horn again. Garry's outline appeared behind the window in the front door. He signaled he

27

would be right out. A couple of minutes later, he finally slid in beside me. "Sorry about that!" he said.

I nodded grimly and started to drive away.

By the time we got to Meijer's it was raining so hard I could hardly see through the windshield with the wipers on high. "Would you mind dropping me off at the door?" Garry suggested.

"Sorry," I replied with icy pleasantness. "You're going to need to know where I'm parked. I don't have an umbrella, so I'm going to stay in the car."

The closest parking spot was about three hundred feet from the door. I stopped, let Garry out, then sat in the car waiting. He said it would take him "just a minute."

That "minute" soon turned into ten. *Where is this guy?* There was no radio in the car, so all I had was my own angry thoughts to keep me company. I drummed out my irritation on the dashboard. Fifteen minutes passed. Twenty. *What's he doing?*

I decided to go in after him. I found him standing in the checkout line with two eight-foot boards.

"What's going on?" I demanded, trying to keep my voice from cracking with anger.

"Oh!" he moaned. "I came in, and there weren't any decent boards. I had to find a clerk. . . ." He told me his tale of woe.

Suddenly I realized just how long his boards really were. "How do you think we're supposed to carry those things?" I snapped. "They won't fit in my trunk!"

"Oh!" he said cheerily, "we can lift out your back seat and put them through from the trunk into the main part of the car."

"What?" I couldn't believe his gall.

"The back of your back seat lifts out. If we put it in the trunk, the boards will fit through."

I'd never heard of such a thing before and it sounded like a horrendous job, but I realized it was the only way we would get the boards home. "I guess I'll go and try to get the seat out," I said.

I turned and walked out of the store as fast as I could. Inside, I was churning. It seemed he expected an awful lot from me! In my mind, I chewed him out: *You want me to take you to Meijer's "just so you can pick up a couple pieces of wood." Then you want me to drop you off at the door so you won't get wet. Then you make me wait for half an hour and get wet by coming in to get you. And now you want me to rip my car apart!*

By the time he arrived, I was soaked, but the back seat was where it had always been. Garry instructed me in the finer points of removing the back seat of a '66 Mustang. Ten minutes later we were loaded up and on our way home. I didn't say a word and neither did he.

When we got to his house, I stepped out of the car, went around back, slid the boards out of the trunk, and handed them over. As I slammed the lid of the trunk I said (hoping he wouldn't say yes), "You need some help getting them into the house?"

"No, thanks. I've got 'em!" He turned to go in. "Thanks for taking me," he said.

"Yeah," I muttered as I slid into the driver's seat.

Unequal Blessing

As I drove away that night I began to think about how I'd treated Garry. *What would I have done if he had been Carole?* I wondered. *What if he had been a girl instead of a guy?*

I knew what I would have done. We could have been in the midst of the worst blizzard in history. If Carole had called, I would have said, "Sure! I'll take you." And I would have had no bad attitudes. None at all. *Such a privilege!* I would have been eager to be of service.

- I wouldn't have hit the horn and waited in the car for Carole to come out. I would have gallantly walked to the door in order to escort her to the car.

- When I found out she wasn't ready to go, I would have laughed lightly as I sat down in a chair to wait. "Take your time!" I would have said when she shouted her apology from the room where she was preparing herself.

- When we arrived at the store, I would have dropped her off at the door without her even having to suggest I do such a thing.

- I would have parked the car and gone inside immediately no matter how wet I would have become.

- If the wood wasn't perfect and she was willing to settle for less, I would have insisted we spend whatever time was necessary in order to get her the quality she deserved.

- Had I known the seat could lift out, I would have joked about having to rip the car apart in order to get the boards in.

- When we arrived back at her house, I wouldn't have asked if she needed help; I would have insisted. "Why don't you run on in and I'll bring the wood. . . ."

- When she told me thanks for the help I had given her, I would have been enthusiastic: "Oh, *no* problem! *Any* time! I'm *happy* to do it!"

And the most amazing thing is that I would have meant it, every word. I would have been happy to do just about anything for Carole. But for Garry. . . .

Loving as Jesus Loved

I was uncomfortable as I drove home that night. I sensed there was something wrong in the way I had acted, something inconsistent between what I professed to be—what I professed to *believe*—and the way I had treated Garry.

In 1 Corinthians 12, God says He has placed the members of the body (the church) together so that "there should be no division in the body, but that its parts should have equal concern for each other" (v. 25). I certainly hadn't shown concern for Garry that equaled my concern for Carole!

Jesus commanded His disciples to "Love one another. . . . All men will know that you are my disciples if you love one another" (John 13:34–35). I realized that if the way I had treated Garry was unloving, then I had failed to obey Jesus and done a poor job of proving my discipleship. That, I sensed, was bad enough. But it got worse.

"This is the message you heard from the beginning," said the Apostle John. "We should love one another. . . . If anyone says, 'I love God,' yet hates his brother, he is a liar. For anyone who does not love his brother, whom he has seen, cannot love God, whom he has not seen. And he has given us this command: Whoever loves God must also love his brother" (1 John 3:11, 4:20–21). I realized that if I had failed to love Garry, then I had not only failed to obey Jesus and prove my discipleship, but I had failed to love Jesus. I was on the skittering edge of proving that I was no Christian at all.

"Well," I told myself, not wanting to be condemned by what I'd done, "maybe my problem is not that I failed to love Garry. Maybe my problem is that I love Carole too *much*. I'm involved in a form of 'hyper-love.'"

Yes, I thought, *that is a possibility*. I'd "over-loved" more than one person in my lifetime. But what comfort could that idea give me if I was supposed to have equal concern for all my brothers and sisters? And anyway, when I got right down to it, "hyper-love" was hardly my problem. Not here. Not in my treatment of Garry. What really bothered me was not that I would have treated Carole better in similar circumstances, but that I had treated Garry so poorly. And not only that, but I would have treated anyone like Garry—anyone in whom I had no romantic interest—equally badly.

I remembered what Jesus said about love: "As I have loved you, so you must love one another" (John 13:34b). Not only that, but, "Love your enemies, do good to those who hate you, bless those who curse you, pray for those who mistreat you" (Luke 6:27–28). And I wasn't even talking about an enemy! Garry was my friend!

"Greater love has no one than this, that one lay down his life for his friends," Jesus said (John 15:13). *Lay down my life?* I wasn't willing to lay down an hour! Yet it was to this kind of love that

God had called me. "My command is this," said Jesus, "Love each other as I have loved you" (John 15:12).

I knew I had no right to treat Garry the way I'd treated him. There was no question about it: I was weak in the area of loving as Jesus loved. My rotten attitude and the rotten feelings I was stuck with afterward helped me realize I had no right to claim I loved one person with undying, self-sacrificing love when I did not at the same time love everyone else the same way. Jesus' love—the love I've been commanded to emulate—is a love for all people. He didn't merely love His latest "flame." He didn't die on the cross because He had some starry-eyed, weak-kneed feelings. He loved with a love that was constant and committed even "unto death."

I came to a conclusion that night: I'm not allowed to treat my brothers worse than I do my sisters. I have no right to treat any-one with less honor or respect or self-sacrifice than Jesus gave me. And so I had an obligation, and still do: not to reduce the quality of my service to Carole so that I would treat her as poorly as I did Garry. Rather, I had to improve my service to Garry and my other brothers and sisters so I would treat them as well as I would treat Carole.

I formulated two rules for myself as a result of the things I discovered that night:

> *Rule 1:* I will treat people in whom I have no romantic interest no worse than I treat people in whom I do have a romantic interest.

> *Rule 2:* I will treat members of the opposite sex no bet-ter than I treat members of my own sex.

Later I realized that this principle of equal concern means that there should be no difference between the way I treat members of the opposite sex before I'm married and the way I treat them after either one is married. On what legitimate grounds could I make such a distinction? When Sarita and I married, my sisters in the flesh and I didn't suddenly find that certain activities we'd engaged in prior to my marriage were unacceptable, immoral, or wrong. I didn't speak to my sisters differently or approach them differently than I did before Sarita and I married. The fact that I'm married gives me no right to alter the quality of my service to members of the body to whom I'm not married.

And so I formulated two more rules of conduct:

> *Rule 3:* I will do nothing with members of the opposite sex now, while we are unmarried, that we cannot continue to do in good conscience later, after one or the other of us has married someone else.

> *Rule 4:* I will do nothing with members of the opposite sex now, while we are unmarried, that I cannot continue to do for the rest of my life with the person I eventually do marry.

This last insight, I think, is especially remarkable. I am amazed how often single men will go out of their way to make good impressions upon women whom they think they might like to marry. They'll spend money, squander time and energy, do almost anything to convince these women to marry them. But how often these same men, once they are married, treat their wives with little honor or respect! They come home from work, plop themselves in front of the TV, and grouse about their wives' poor cooking.

"Well, what can you expect?" people say. I think we can expect that men who want to follow the Lord will treat their wives no worse than they treated the women they dated! When a man marries, he pledges himself to love his wife with a special love, a committed love, a love of top priority—"You are the one I will love first, before all others"—not with a love that takes for granted, ignores, and despises. I find no legitimate grounds in

Scripture for a man to treat the women he's dating *better* than he expects to treat his wife!

Treating Each Other with Equal Concern

If one decides to treat members of both sexes with equal concern; if one determines that being married should make no difference in the way one treats members of the opposite sex, how does this affect one's behavior? The implications are far-reaching.

In the Area of Finance

If you treat all your brothers and sisters with equal concern, you're not going to spend more on a date than you can legitimately afford.

Most people I know would never wipe out their savings accounts for members of their own sex. A married couple with a good relationship will also avoid destroying their financial stability in hopes of somehow making a good impression on one another. So, too, with brothers and sisters.

I know of no man who will call a male friend, ask if his friend would like to go to a movie, and then, without saying anything, as a matter of course and expectation, pay his friend's way. I know of no man who, having received an invitation to go to a movie with a male friend, will expect his friend to pay his way. But I know women who expect men to pay their way. And I know men who expect women to let them pay. Why? Why should brothers or sisters do these kinds of things with, to, or for members of the opposite sex? Brothers and sisters shouldn't. And they don't. Instead, they show as much concern for each other's finances as they do for their own.

A brother may offer to pay his sister's way, and a sister may offer to pay her brother's way. In brother-sister relationships there's no rule that "the guy pays for the girl" or that "each one pays for himself." If a brother is as poor as I was when I was single, he won't offer to pay his sister's way. And if a sister is poor, she won't offer to pay her brother's way. If they're going to do something that costs money, they'll pay for themselves. On the other hand, more likely even than this, the question of money won't come up. Brothers and sisters who are short on money will know and understand each other's financial needs, so they will do what they can to avoid dates that cost money. Since they don't need an excuse, some costly event that provides a reason for a date, they'll do things that cost nothing at all.

In the Area of Asking People for Dates

There's no rule in relationships between brothers and sisters that says "girls don't call guys." Men call other men; women call other women. Husbands and wives initiate calls one to the other. Brothers and sisters call each other as well.

If a sister wants to spend time with her brother, she'll call him up. Why should she wait till he calls? If she's lonely or hurting or wants a male friend to provide perspective or insight on an issue, why shouldn't she call her brother? If a brother feels in need of female companionship, he'll call his sister. *Why shouldn't she call him?* I believe she should. Indeed, I believe Scripture encourages her to do just that (see chapter 8).

And so brothers and sisters call each other up, as much for the pleasure of conversation as for arranging future dates.

᙭ ᙭ ᙭

One afternoon late in spring, I was tired of studying and called Mary. "You want to go for a bike ride with me? I need a break."

"Oh!" she said, "I'd love to, but I'm really too busy."

"Hmmm," I said. I knew her roommate, Debbie. "Is Debbie there?"

"Hold on a second."

Debbie came to the phone. She wasn't available, either. I don't remember who I went out with; it may have been a guy.

What I did to Mary—calling her for a date, then asking for her roommate—is not the kind of thing a guy would do to a girl he wants to impress with his special concern. But it's the kind of thing a brother will do to his sister or a friend will do to a friend.

Brothers and sisters don't call each other up to ask for dates in order to demonstrate unequal concern, but to show plain, ordinary, *loving* concern. If I call you up and you're not able at the moment to receive my ministrations, then I'll seek someone else to bless.

Not so long ago, I was traveling along the Atlantic seaboard. I visited one of my sisters (one of my biological sisters) in Boston. She invited me to go with her to her favorite ice cream parlor.

"Oh!" I said wistfully, "I'm really short of funds. . . ."

"Don't worry about that!" Ruth said. "It's my treat! I want you to see this place."

So we went on a date, my sister and I. She invited. And she paid—for both of us.

That's the way it is with brothers and sisters—biological brothers and sisters and spiritual brothers and sisters. The brother may initiate; the sister may initiate. The brother may pay; the sister may pay. They may pay for themselves or they may pay for each other.

In General

In sum, brothers and sisters in the Lord do the kinds of friendly things biological brothers and sisters are supposed to do. They avoid the activities that men and women who are courting often engage in to win each other's hands in marriage. They don't tell each other that they are "friends" and then put their arms around each other, hug, kiss, and touch each other in the manner of boyfriends and girlfriends. They don't flirt with one another, "make eyes" at one another, or show each other special solicitude. They don't do anything with, to, or for members of the opposite sex that they wouldn't do for members of their own . . . unless the situation specifically demands that kind of special attention or behavior.

People have challenged me on this point. "Are you suggesting we drop all chivalry, that guys aren't supposed to open doors for girls anymore? . . . Things like that?"

No. That's not what I'm saying. I think courtesy and thoughtfulness—chivalry, as some call it—is a wonderful thing. It fits well with the Biblical mandate to "consider others better than [yourself]" (Philippians 2:3). What I'm suggesting is that, if you're a guy, and, when you drive, you normally go around to the other side of the car to open the door for your female passengers, then you ought to be just as considerate of your passengers who are male. Why shouldn't you open the door for them, too? That's a form of consideration, a form of caring. If you don't like this suggestion, then I challenge you: Are there Scriptural grounds for showing your brothers less care and concern than you show your sisters? I know of none. On what basis, then, will you show your sisters more consideration than you do your brothers?

The father of a teenage girl once told me, "I have always taught my daughter that when a young man takes her out, she is not only to *allow* him to open the car door for her, she is to *wait* for him to do so. And when he lets her into the car, she is *not* to lean across the front seat to unlock his door for him. He should do that for himself."

And I ask: Why?

I don't have a problem with a sister allowing her brother to open the door for her. I don't begrudge men showing that kind of special consideration for their sisters. But Scripture tells us to serve one another (Galatians 5:13). Is there a Scriptural reason, then, why a sister ought *not* to serve her brother by leaning across to open his door for him? Why should she refuse to serve him in that way?

But perhaps we're missing the main point. These, really, are petty issues. My concern is not so much with activities that can be interpreted solely as matters of chivalry and politeness; my concern is with activities that tend to communicate implications of commitment (see chapters 4 through 6): the bouquets of flowers, the friendship cards, the "knowing" glances, and back rubs.

If brothers or sisters find they want to do special things for a certain member of the opposite sex more readily than they would normally do such things for members of their own, they ask themselves: "Do I love members of my own sex enough? Do I need, perhaps, to turn down this opportunity to love this member of the opposite sex until I've learned to love members of my own sex better?" It's the same kind of question a husband should ask himself if he's ever attracted to a woman other than his wife: "Do I love my own wife enough? Do I need, perhaps, to turn down this opportunity to show consideration for this other woman until I've learned to love my wife better?"

The thing in itself, the activity this husband or brother is considering, may be perfectly legitimate. There may be no reason, on its own merits, that the activity needs to be avoided. There's nothing wrong with smiling at a person, is there? What's the matter with giving a person a flower or a friendship card? Quite possibly, nothing at all. But would you do these things for a member of your own sex? *Are* you doing them for members of your own sex? Are you doing these things—supposing you're married—for your husband or wife? Are you being honest when you say you're "just being friendly" or "just treating him like a brother?" If you're not doing this activity with, to, or for at least one member of your own sex, you're probably doing something brothers and sisters shouldn't be involved in.

I often used this rule of equality as a means to harness some of my romantic drives for good. For several years I made it my habit not to write to the "woman of my dreams" (whoever she happened to be) unless I had first written to some of my other friends. This discipline encouraged me to love my friends better than I would have loved them otherwise, and it enabled me to avoid the temptation of "over-loving" the woman who made my heart throb.

Indeed, I believe this principle of showing equal concern may be the practical basis for almost everything that follows in this book. If you treat all members of the body with equal concern, you will not feel stifled in your relations with members of the opposite sex. You will express yourself openly, honestly, and transparently. You will avoid game playing—trying to project yourself as being something other than what you are. You will not become involved in physical-sexual intimacy or ownership relationships.

When you show equal concern for all members of the body, it means you will engage in a wider range of activities than you would otherwise. You will see your brothers and sisters in a broader range of times and contexts than you would if you were "going together." You will relate to—bless and be blessed by—a larger number of people than you would otherwise. You will act consistently at all times. You will get to know others and let them get to know you. Finally, in the best way possible, you will be preparing yourself to fulfill the responsibilities of a marriage commitment.

Questions for Study and Discussion

1. If no one used the term *brother-sister relationship* or spoke of spiritual *brothers* and *sisters*, would there still be scriptural grounds for the idea of treating members of the opposite sex no better or worse than you treat members of your own? (Look up Matthew 7:12, Luke 10:25-37, and Leviticus 19:18.) Discuss your feelings on the matter.

2. Many people object to the principle laid out in this chapter. Those with a philosophical bent say, "It's impossible to treat everyone identically. You *live closer* to some people than you do to others. By reason of work, school, or other common interests, you're going to naturally tend to *spend more time* with some people than you do with others. You *like* some people better than you do others. The fact that Western countries have better news services and communication facilities means that, even if you wanted to know what is happening to brothers and sisters in other countries, you will be *more aware* of what is happening to your brothers and sisters in the West than of what is happening to believers in other parts of the world."

Those with a more practical orientation keep the discussion focused on male-female relationships. "You can't help treating members of the opposite sex differently," they say. "We are different. God made us that way. We respond differently both emotionally and physically. So, since God made us as we are—different—I don't believe He expects us to treat everyone the same."

a. God obviously *did* make us different from each other, and He knows our limitations as human beings (among others, that we are neither omniscient nor omnipresent and that we have emotions). What, then, does He mean when He says "there should be no division in the body, but . . . its parts should have equal concern for each other. If one part suffers, every part suffers with it; if one part is honored, every part rejoices with it" (1 Corinthians 12:25–26)? Practically speaking, how can you put this principle into practice? (Luke 10:25–37 may provide a little help in answering this question.)

b. Among those toward whom you could demonstrate the love of Jesus and equal concern, have you been doing so? Why or why not?

3. The distinctions we make between the sexes often have nothing to do with our limitations as human beings; they have everything to do with our desires.

Below is a list of things that men and women will often do for one another. Decide whether or not it is legitimate for a member of your sex to engage in these activities. If you're female, answer the questions from your perspective. If you're male, answer from a male's perspective. When are these activities legitimate? When are they not? Explain your answers.

a. Invite a member of the opposite sex to go to a movie.

b. Pay for your opposite-sex friend's ticket to the movie.

c. Hold the door open for a member of the opposite sex.

d. Fix an opposite-sex friend's car.

e. Wash an opposite-sex friend's clothes.

f. Carry an opposite-sex friend's books.

g. Lend money to a friend of the opposite sex.

h. Hold hands with, hug, or kiss a member of the opposite sex.

i. Give a back rub to a member of the opposite sex.

4. What might motivate a person to do the kinds of things listed above in question 3? Which motives are Biblically acceptable? Which are Biblically unacceptable?

5. Formulate a general rule about when it is legitimate to make a distinction between the sexes in the way you treat them. In what circumstances are such distinctions legitimate? When are they illegitimate? Explain why you believe as you do.

6. A married woman wrote an editorial in a secular newspaper. She said she never wears a wedding band. At first this was because her husband couldn't afford to buy her one. Now she doesn't wear one *on principle*. She believes that, if she were to wear a wedding band, she would miss out on too many significant and stimulating conversations. "Single men (and married men 'on the prowl') don't approach married women," she explained.

By refusing to wear a ring, men don't know that she's married. Over the years, many men have come up and initiated conversations with her—men who later admitted that they would have never approached her had she been wearing a ring. She described a number of significant relationships she has enjoyed as a result of this ploy.

Few people will argue that this woman's observations are correct: people tend to treat marrieds differently than they do unmarrieds. How does the brother-sister principle of equality bear upon this issue?

a. For what legitimate reasons should members of the opposite sex avoid conversations with married people?

b. For what legitimate reasons should you ever avoid conversing with someone who is not on your list of hot prospects for a romantic relationship ("too young," "too old," "too ——," "not interested")?

c. What advantages, disadvantages, and dangers might there be in married people doing what this woman did: presenting themselves as if they were unmarried?

d. What advantages, disadvantages, and dangers might there be in married people openly acknowledging their married state but actively *pursuing* significant conversations with singles?

e. What advantages, disadvantages, and dangers might there be in single people actively pursuing significant conversations with marrieds?

f. How does your behavior need to change in this area—and *why*?

7. In their wedding vows, husbands and wives commit themselves to treat each other differently than they treat any other human beings on the face of the earth.

a. To what specific behaviors do they commit themselves?

b. Having committed themselves to these behaviors, can they still show equal concern for other members of the body? Why or why not?

c. Are the commitments husbands and wives make legitimate? Why or why not?

8. Boyfriends, girlfriends, and "serious" daters generally tend to treat each other differently than they treat other members of the body of Christ.

   a. Describe the specific kinds of behaviors boyfriends, girlfriends, and "serious" couples engage in that they will not engage in with others.

   b. On what grounds do they make the distinctions between themselves and other members of the body? Are they legitimate grounds (and, therefore, legitimate distinctions)? Why or why not?

9. Is it possible to have a boyfriend-girlfriend or "serious" dating relationship and to show equal concern for all members of the body of Christ? Why or why not?

10. Have you ever known someone who was hurt because someone else demonstrated unequal concern for members of the body? Describe the situation.

11. Suppose you were to discipline yourself to demonstrate equal concern for all your brothers and sisters.

    a. Compared with the way you tend to act now, how would your behavior be different when you meet someone who:

    - is shy?
    - dresses poorly?
    - has bad breath or noticeable body odor?
    - is relatively homely?
    - exhibits other characteristics that tend to make him or her a social outcast?

    b. What does Matthew 25:31–46 have to say about this subject?

    c. If you were to change your behavior as we have described,

- What kind of role would you likely find yourself playing within the larger group of which you are now a part?

- How would your behavior be viewed by group "insiders"?

- How would it be viewed by the people who tend to be social outcasts?

- What difference might it make in the lives of those who have always been outcasts?

12. How will you ensure that your relationships with members of the opposite sex will help rather than hinder you in showing equal concern for other members of the body of Christ?

Do not lie. Do not deceive one another.

Leviticus 19:11

Simply let your "Yes" be "Yes," and your "No," "No"; anything beyond this comes from the evil one.

Matthew 5:37

For by your words you will be acquitted, and by your words you will be condemned.

Matthew 12:37

3

SPEAKING THE TRUTH IN LOVE

Brothers and Sisters Speak the Truth in Love

One day several weeks after Sarita and I first talked about being brother and sister, I was eating lunch with the gang in Landon Hall. Sarita was there, too. At one point in the conversation, I found myself wanting to say something about what I'd done the previous evening with Mary, a girl from my dorm in whom I had a strong romantic interest. I hesitated for a moment, however, because I realized I was about to tell the story in a way that was slightly different from how I would have told it had Sarita not been present. Instead of saying, "Last night, this girl from my dorm and I . . . ," I wanted to say, "Last night, this friend of mine and I. . . ." I would have gone on to substitute the word *friend* wherever I would have otherwise said *Mary* or *girl*.

You're probably familiar with this ploy. Maybe you've used it yourself. I wanted to hide the fact that my *friend* happened to be a member of the opposite sex. Why? *Because Sarita was there.* Sarita was romantically interested in me. Mary was not. I'm sure some-

47

where in the recesses of my mind I must have reasoned that it was possible nothing would ever come of my relationship with Mary: *She's not that interested in me. On the other hand, Sarita is. Why should I jeopardize my chances with Sarita? I don't need to mention Mary or the fact that I was out with another girl.*

It was almost unconscious. I certainly hadn't thought about it long and hard.

But then I thought, *Is that being totally honest?*

I had to admit it was not.

What if Sarita were my biological sister: would I hide Mary's identity from her?

Again I had to admit: No. One of my biological sisters would have no aversion to the idea of my spending an evening with the other. If one of my sisters happened to know I had been out with the other the night before, she would ask: "How did it go?" And when I told her, she would be pleased that we had had a good time.

I continued my self-examination: *Is there a legitimate reason not to admit the truth? Any valid purpose for not telling the group (including Sarita) that what I am about to say is the result of my having spent time with another sister?*

I could come up with no valid reasons to hide the truth. The reason I wanted to obscure Mary's identity was selfish in nature. It would be no blessing to Sarita for me to hide the fact I'd been out with another woman. All it could do is possibly help me string Sarita along—make her think I was more interested in her than I really was. And stringing someone along is not exactly the most honorable endeavor!

If anything, if I were to avoid telling Sarita about Mary, I would be impoverishing Sarita by founding our relationship on a lie and limiting the amount of information I could pass on to her.

"I will not do anything with, to, or for you that I would not do with, to, or for my own sister," I had told Sarita. I had committed myself to treat her as my sister. I knew what I had to do if I was to fulfill that promise.

"Last night, Mary, this girl from my dorm, and I . . . ," I began.

Sarita's jaw dropped about an inch when she heard those words. Disappointment and jealous curiosity were etched across her face: *Who is this other woman?*

Brothers and Sisters Use No Guile

In John 1:47, Jesus describes His soon-to-be disciple Nathanael as a man in whom there is "no guile" (KJV, RSV) or "nothing false" (NIV). I like that idea: *no guile; nothing false.*

Webster's *New World Dictionary of the American Language* defines *guile* as "slyness and cunning in dealing with others." Jesus tells us to conduct our affairs without guile. In Matthew 5:37, He says, "Simply let your 'Yes' be 'Yes,' and your 'No,' 'No'; anything beyond this comes from the evil one."

Yes, there are times for slyness and cunning. Jesus tells us to be "as shrewd as snakes" when we are among the "wolves" of this world (Matthew 10:16). But that day in the cafeteria as I contemplated what to say to the group, I was hardly a sheep in the presence of a Sarita wolf! And brothers and sisters who are seeking to bless each other are not and never should be wolves to one another.

Sarita was my friend. That's what she had professed to be. And I'd professed to be her friend as well. On what grounds did I think I needed to be cunning or sly?

I had no legitimate reason to try to hide Mary's gender or identity. I was hurting no one by spending time with her. Mary had hurt no one by spending time with me. Indeed, if we had hurt someone by spending time together, then we would have needed to repent of our behavior and to ask the person who was hurt for his or her forgiveness! Whether our behavior was legitimate or illegitimate, Mary and I had no right to cover it up.

If I had spoken of Mary as merely "a friend," I would have been doing so strictly because I wanted to mislead Sarita, to give her the impression or allow her to think that I had no interests in other women.

But I did have interests in other women! And I spent time with them and enjoyed my relationships with them. They were a blessing to me, and I did my best to be a blessing to them.

In Leviticus 19:11, God tells His people, "Do not lie. Do not deceive one another." Brothers and sisters should have no reason to deceive each other. If they are somehow failing to bless each other, then they need to admit it, confess their sin and be made right with one another. If they are *not* failing to bless each other—in other words, if they *are* blessing each other to the best of their abilities, then they have no reason to be ashamed of their behavior, and the truth should be no cause of pain.

The truth was that I had gone out with Mary. I had been out with her before and I intended to spend time with her in the future. Moreover, the reason I had gone out with Mary and the reason I was interested in talking about what we had done arose from no spiteful or hurtful desires. I liked Mary and wanted to bless her. I liked Sarita, too, and wanted to bless her just as much as I was blessing Mary.

True, I happened to be more romantically attracted to Mary at the time. But that made no difference in the way I treated her. It should have made no difference in the way I related to Sarita either. I had openly committed myself to both women to treat them as my sisters: with equal concern, for the purpose of blessing them. That was all that should have mattered.

Brothers and Sisters Walk Consistently

A friend of mine, Doug, said he and LeAnn were romantically interested in each other but had committed themselves to treat each other as brother and sister. They were students at a small Christian college. "The problem is," he said, "on our campus, as soon as a guy and girl show any interest in one another—if they go out together even once—they're branded. Everyone says, 'They're going together.' It's like you're cut off from contact with anyone else.

"What I'd like to know," he said, "is how do you avoid people putting you into a box like that? The pressure is awful!"

"How have you tried to avoid it?" I asked.

He told me that he and LeAnn had come up with the idea of going out for walks after dark. That way no one would see them together, or if they were seen together, from a distance no one would be able to recognize them.

"There's something wrong with that strategy," I said. "You're being inconsistent. Even if other people never see you together and never label you as a couple, by your sneaking out together, you're treating each other differently than you would your own brother or sister. You wouldn't go sneaking out after dark to go for a walk with your physical brother or sister! Why should you do that with LeAnn? You're letting the opinions and misperceptions of the people around you shape the way you treat your sister. *Don't do it!*"

As Romans 12:2 puts it, "Don't be conformed to this world" (RSV), or, in the Phillips translation: "Don't let the world squeeze you into its mold." Rather, be *transformed*. Not only be transformed yourself, but *help transform your world*. Coming out and publicly showing the kind of relationship they have can be one of the greatest ministries a brother and sister engage in. Paul told Timothy to "set an example for the believers" (1 Timothy 4:12). Brothers and sisters seek to do just that.

"It seems to me, the solution to your problem is not to retreat and hide, but to confront it head-on," I told Doug. "Demonstrate the kind of relationship you have. Talk about it. Explain what you're doing and why. I don't think you have to worry so much about denying the accusations of your friends or trying to give them fewer opportunities to see the two of you together. What you need is to make the positive statement: 'We have more friends than just one another. We *want* more friends than just each other. We want to bless our friends. We want to show equal concern for all members of the body. Yes, we spend time together. Yes, we have a romantic interest in each other. But those things are not as important as the commitment we have made to treat each other as brother and sister . . . and to continue to treat each other as brother and sister until the time should come—*if* such a time should ever come—when we feel called to marry each other.'

"You need to make it clear to people that at this time the two of you have no special commitments to one another—no greater *number* of commitments and no more *special* commitments—than you have to anyone else."

Brothers and sisters refuse to let the crowd squeeze them into the world's mold. No matter how, when, or where one observes them, brothers' and sisters' lives hang together. Brothers and sisters are honest; they walk consistently; they conduct their affairs with integrity.

Brothers and Sisters
Speak the Truth in Love—Even When it Hurts

I have worked with the brother-sister model of male-female relationships for over fifteen years now. I have become convinced that brother-sister relationships offer every legitimate advantage that other types of premarital and extramarital relationships (boyfriend-girlfriend relationships, "serious" relationships, etc.) offer. You cannot find a single benefit in these other relationships that you cannot also find in brother-sister relationships.

I was once speaking to a college group where I made that claim. A young man came to me afterward and said, "I think I know a benefit that brother-sister relationships don't offer. When you're in a 'serious' relationship, there's a pressure on you to continue with the relationship. So, whereas in a brother-sister relationship you can ignore your brother's or sister's faults, in a boyfriend-girlfriend or 'serious' relationship, when someone does something that bugs you, you've got to deal with it. You can't just let things slide. That means you're likely to mature a lot faster if you get involved in boyfriend-girlfriend or 'serious' relationships than if you just stick with just being brother and sister."

His reasoning sounded solid. The psychology of it all made sense. I thought maybe he had come up with a benefit to these other kinds of relationships.

But then I remembered: Brothers and sisters obey their Father's commands, no matter how difficult. Though *psychologically* it may be easier to confront a boyfriend or girlfriend or someone else with whom we feel obligated to keep "going" together, God makes it very clear: when we recognize a sin, we are under obligation to go to our brother or sister and make it right. It doesn't matter if it's easy or not, the command is "Go!"

"If you are offering your gift at the altar and there remember that your brother has something against you," Jesus said, "leave your gift there in front of the altar. First go and be reconciled to your brother; then come and offer your gift" (Matthew 5:23–24).

In Matthew 18:15ff, He said, "If your brother sins against you, go and show him his fault, just between the two of you. If he listens to you, you have won your brother over." On the other hand, if he *won't* listen to you, then you're still not off the hook. You have the responsibility to follow up even further: "take one or two others along, so that 'every matter may be established by the testimony of two or three witnesses.'" Eventually, if our brother is totally hardened in his sin, we are told to take the matter before the church.

But the point is, we are not free to avoid communicating with our brothers and sisters just because it may be difficult or painful. If our speech may bless them, if it could build them up (see Ephesians 4:29), show them the error of their ways or help them to see a better way, brothers and sisters recognize they have an inescapable responsibility to speak.

As the Lord said to Ezekiel in Ezekiel 3:17–21:

Son of man, I have made you a watchman for the house of Israel; so hear the word I speak and give them warning from me. When I say to a wicked man, "You will surely die," and you do not warn him or speak out to dissuade him from his evil ways . . . , that wicked man will die for his sin, and I will hold you accountable for his blood. But if you do warn the wicked man and he does not turn from his wickedness or from his evil ways, he will die for his sin; but you will have saved yourself.

Again, when a righteous man turns from his righteousness and does evil, and I put a stumbling block before him, he will die. Since you did not warn him, he will die for his sin. . . . I will hold you accountable for his blood. But if you do warn the righteous man not to sin and he does not sin, he will surely live because he took warning, and you will have saved yourself.

Brothers and sisters speak the truth even when it hurts. David Augsburger calls it "caring enough to confront" or "care-fronting," "truthing it in love."[1] Brothers and sisters do not speak *to* hurt, but if pain must come in order for good to be done, they don't shy away from saying what needs to be said.

"Truth and love are the two necessary ingredients for any relationship with integrity," says Augsburger.

Love—because all positive relationships begin with friendship, appreciation, respect. And truth—because no relationship of trust can long grow from dishonesty, deceit, betrayal; it springs up from the solid stuff of integrity. . . .

These are the two arms of genuine relationship: Confrontation with truth; affirmation with love.

I grow most rapidly when supported with the arm of loving respect, then confronted with the arm of clear honesty. Confronting and caring stimulate growth.[2]

Brothers and sisters care enough to confront. They speak the truth in love. They are the friends whose wounds, though painful, are faithful and much to be desired above the sweet kisses of flattering enemies (Proverbs 27:6).

The Benefits of Being Honest

Despite the cost of walking with integrity and the difficulty of maintaining our honesty, my sisters and I came to rejoice in the freedom that was ours as a result of our being able to tell each other what we really thought and felt.

We never had to hide the fact that we were going out with other people. If anything, we rejoiced in one another's dates. If one of my sisters had a good date with another brother, I was as thrilled as she was. If the guy she'd gone out with was a boor, I was just as disappointed or angry, often even more than she was. ("Him thinking he could treat my sister like that!")

I was genuinely interested in my sisters as people, not merely as potential wife material. My primary concern was not whether I would get married to this or that sister, but whether my sisters were being blessed. I wanted to make sure that they were.

Brothers and sisters have no reason to pretend or claim that they have not spent time with other members of the opposite sex when, in fact, they have.

They have no reason to claim a particular conversation was only mildly interesting to them when, in fact, it was one of the most stimulating interchanges they have had in years. They have no reason to claim they have no interest in other members of the opposite sex when, in fact, there is a person who is becoming increasingly fascinating to them.

I became a trusted confidant to many of my sisters, someone with whom they shared their deepest secrets and to whom they looked for wise advice. This occurred largely because I was interested in them as whole people and because I was committed to telling the truth and living my life without guile.

Being brother and sister together, reminding ourselves of that fact, and making a commitment to conduct our affairs with integrity made it easier not only for Sarita and me, but for all my brothers and sisters and me to get to know each other well, as friends know their friends, and brothers and sisters know their siblings. We came to know each other in the inner recesses of our spirits, the quality of our characters, the outer reaches of our minds. And to the same extent that we came to know each other well, my brothers and sisters and I became well prepared for marriage.

Questions for Study and Discussion

1. Suppose you were to deliberately hide from a "special" brother or sister the fact that you spend time with other brothers or sisters. On the few occasions that you do happen to tell this person about your relationships with other people, you always *scrub* your speech to make it gender-neutral. Thus, instead of "he said" or "she said," you say, "this friend of mine," "*they* said," etc.

   a. What benefits would such a plan offer you? What benefits would it offer that "special" brother or sister toward whom you act this way?

   b. What problems would such a plan present?

   c. What potential costs might you or your brother or sister have to pay if you were to work this plan?

   d. What does 1 Corinthians 13:5 and 6—"[Love] is not self-seeking. . . . Love . . . rejoices with the truth"—have to say about this plan?

2. How honest are you in your relationships with members of the opposite sex?

   a. Describe a situation where you were more honest with a member of the opposite sex than you'd originally intended to be. What were the costs? What were the benefits?

   b. Describe a conversation with a member of the opposite sex in which you were less than fully honest about your thoughts or feelings. What happened as a result of that dishonesty? In the end, was your relationship helped or hurt by your act(s) of dishonesty?

   c. List five ways you've been tempted to be dishonest with a member of the opposite sex. (For example, "When I was talking with a girl I liked, I tried to hide the fact that Karla, a girl I'd been out with, was a girl."

"Even though we'd just had a great conversation, I ignored Richard when he walked by me in the hall because I was with my boyfriend.")

3. What would motivate you to withhold the truth from a member of the opposite sex? Are any of these motives good, righteous, pure? Are any of them tainted with evil, unrighteousness, or impurity?

4. According to Revelation 3:19, what is one way Jesus demonstrates His love toward us? How can you show similar love to your brothers and sisters?

If a person thoughtlessly takes an oath to do anything, whether good or evil—in any matter one might carelessly swear about— even though he is unaware of it, in any case when he learns of it he will be guilty.

Leviticus 5:4

It is better not to vow than to make a vow and not fulfill it. Do not let your mouth lead you into sin. And do not protest to the temple messenger, "My vow was a mistake." Why should God be angry at what you say and destroy the work of your hands?

Ecclesiastes 5:5–6

4

"UNDER THE TERMS OF THIS CONTRACT . . ."

Brothers and Sisters Refuse to Make Unspoken, Unwanted, Unmeant, Lying Vows

When they first started to date, Grant told Tracy he wanted to be "just friends." Tracy was happy with the arrangement.

But then, after about a month of going out together, their relationship began to change. It happened slowly and seemed natural enough, but there was a small prick in Tracy's conscience when Grant first put his arm around her shoulder and kept it there. Later that evening Tracy wondered again what was happening between them when Grant gave her a good-night kiss. As he gently pulled her to him and touched his lips to hers, the question crossed her mind: *Weren't we going to be 'just friends'?* But then, in the warmth of the moment, she put the thought behind her.

Within a couple of weeks, Grant's and Tracy's physical relationship had moved more clearly into the sexual arena. They weren't merely pecking each other on the mouth. Their kisses lingered. And Grant's hand, which he'd been so careful that first night never to let stray from Tracy's shoulder, now began gliding down to the small of her back, to her side, to her hips. . . .

They never got involved in "heavy" petting, but by gradual increments Grant's and Tracy's physical relationship progressed. And Tracy's comfort, trust, and expectations for their future grew with it. She had all but forgotten Grant's introductory statement when, at the end of a date about seven months into their relationship, he remarked, "Well, Tracy. I've really enjoyed our relationship, but this is going to have to be the last time we see each other for a while. I've begun seeing Brenda."

"Huh?!" said Tracy, startled. "What! What are you saying?"

"Tracy, I told you six months ago that I wanted to be your *friend*," Grant pleaded. "I told you I was making no commitments."

"'No commitments'!" Tracy shouted. "'No commitments'! You. . . !" Tears welled in her eyes as Tracy felt the bitter sting of betrayal. How natural and innocent Grant made it sound: "*I never said . . .*" And yet he *had* said, hadn't he? By his *actions*.

Grant's mistake—was it a mistake?—was only one of many that occur in male-female relationships. Men and women often communicate to one another things they don't intend, don't want, or don't mean to say. Brothers and sisters do everything they can to avoid this kind of duplicity. They refuse to communicate promises they don't mean, want, or intend to fulfill.

Physical Actions Communicate

Ron and Jan had been spending significant time together over the course of several months. They were friends and treated each other as such. But Jan wanted more.

"Ron," she finally burst out one day, "why don't we have a physical relationship? I mean, it's a lot of fun!"

"I know it's a lot of fun," he replied, thinking back to the times he'd spent with his girlfriends in high school kissing and "making out." "But physical contact is a lot more than fun. It communicates. If we were to have a physical relationship, I'd be implying something about my relationship with you. And I don't want to be implying or saying with my actions something that I would never say with words."

Kinesiologists—people who study these things—say that, in a normal, face-to-face conversation, words account for only about a third of what's communicated. Close to two-thirds of everything we say to other people is conveyed by nonverbal means—the way we act, how we dress, our intonation, gestures, how close we come to the other person, etc.[1]

Nonverbal communication is based on inference and implication. We humans generally believe that human actions are meaningful: people do things with a purpose, for a reason. We understand that gifts, gestures, touches, looks, . . . just about every action has significance. And so when we observe someone doing something, we try to interpret it: *Why is he doing that?* We infer, or reason, to a conclusion from what we know: our observations. We see someone grimace and think to ourselves: *He's in pain!* Or, *He ate something sour.* Or, *He's having a heart attack.* We see a man chopping wood in a forest: *He must be a woodcutter.* Or, *He has a wood stove.*

Most people don't do a lot of heavy thinking to come to their conclusions. It's an intuitive process; we do it without the conscious use of reason. But if questioned, most of us are able to give reasonable explanations of why we interpret our observations as we do.

Whether or not we are capable of inferring accurately from what we observe, all human beings do make inferences based on what they see. Therefore, whether or not we mean something by our behavior or intend to say something through our actions, if our actions are observed, we may be sure they will be interpreted. The observer will attach some meaning to what we do.

Brothers and sisters understand this process. They understand that physical actions communicate and that other people will form conclusions about them based on what they observe. Therefore, brothers and sisters realize that if they are to communicate accurately, their words and actions must be congruent; they must

not say one thing by their words and another by their actions. If
their words say one thing and their actions another, someone—
possibly even themselves—will be confused. And once someone
is confused, they are likely to be hurt. Because inconsistency in
speech and conduct is one of the best ways to destroy a friendship, brothers and sisters seek to be consistent at all times.

Brothers and Sisters
Clearly Define Their Commitments

No Inferred or Implied Commitments

God says, "It is better not to vow than to make a vow and not
fulfill it. Do not let your mouth lead you into sin. And do not
protest to the temple messenger, 'My vow was a mistake.' Why
should God be angry at what you say and destroy the work of
your hands?" (Ecclesiastes 5:5–6).

"Simply let your 'Yes' be 'Yes,' and your 'No,' 'No,'" said
Jesus in Matthew 5:37. In other words, let your word be as good
as your oath.

It would be pharisaism in the extreme for us to limit the significance of these verses to spoken words alone. God is not the
kind of God who says, "It is fine to mislead with your actions as
long as your words are true." A false vow is a false vow whether
spoken or acted out.

While I was in college I realized that until I could clarify my
thoughts enough to express them in words, I had no business expressing them in action. It would be sin to imply by my actions
that I was committed to do something if I could not state in
words what I was committed to do.

There are two reasons for this. First, if I wasn't sure what I
was thinking, how could I expect my brothers and sisters to
know for me? If I expressed my thoughts and feelings in action
before being able to express them in words, I would quite likely
open myself to charges of double-dealing, misdirection, and
fraud. Though I may have had no intention to deceive, misdirect,
or defraud, if I acted first and decided later, I might find that my

actions had been inappropriate. The commitment I expressed in action was not the commitment I eventually wanted to make.

Second, even if my actions were consistent with the way I later decided, I would be guilty of acting in a thoughtless manner. I would be guilty of having implied a commitment that I wasn't sure I could, would, or wanted to keep. In other words, I would be guilty of having said, "Yes (maybe)." Or, "Yes (it might turn out this way)." Or, "Yes (I hope)." Or, "Yes (I'd like it to be so)." I would not have said what Jesus commanded me to say: "Yes (yes)" or "No (no)."

"If a person thoughtlessly takes an oath to do anything, whether good or evil . . . even though he is unaware of it, in any case when he learns of it he will be guilty," says God in Leviticus 5:4. *Even though you are unaware of it,* says God, you're guilty. You're guilty not for intentionally vowing *falsely* or vowing something *evil* but for *vowing unintentionally*: for *thoughtlessly taking an oath.*

"Men will have to give account on the day of judgment for every careless word they have spoken," said Jesus (Matthew 12:36). I have an idea He could have included careless actions as well, especially actions that say things that aren't true.

And so I made a rule for myself: I will not say in action, what I cannot honestly say with words; and I will not say in action *until* I've said with words. I did not want to be guilty of implying something false. I did not want to be guilty of conveying a message I was not sure was true. Nor did I want to be guilty of taking an oath unintentionally. I wanted my "Yes" to mean "Yes," and my "No," "No." If I wasn't sure, I would keep my mouth shut and my actions neutral, or I would say I didn't know. But I would never act upon my thoughts or feelings until I was sure what I meant.

Brothers and sisters define their commitments; they refuse to make commitments through inference and implication. They refuse to say in action what they cannot honestly say with words, and they refuse to say in action *until* they've said with words. Brothers and sisters don't want to mislead others, and they don't want to be misled themselves through unintentional, unwanted, or unmeant communication.

Clearly Defined Exit Plans

"Kelly and I are committed to pursuing the possibility of marriage," Jim told me.

"Oh, yeah?" I asked. "What does that mean?"

Jim hadn't considered that question before. Still, he was able to respond quickly: "It means we want to get to know each other. So we'll be spending more time with each other and not so much time with other people. It also means we won't date other people."

"Hmm!" I said. "So how will you get to know each other?"

"By spending time together."

"Uh-huh. And *how much* more time do you intend to spend with one another?" I wanted to bear in on this matter of having a well-defined commitment.

"As I said," Jim replied, "we'll spend more time with one another than we spend with other people."

"Okay. So for *how long* will you spend this 'more time' with one another?"

By this point Jim was becoming irritated. He and I both knew I was pushing him. "We'll spend more time together for as long as it takes us to find out if we're supposed to marry," he said. "It might take four weeks, and it might take four years. We don't know!"

"Hmm. Then *how* will you know—what will *tell* you—that you are or are not supposed to marry?"

Neither Jim nor anyone else with whom I've carried on similar discussions has ever been able to answer this last question. They usually have some vague ideas about what might *disqualify* them from marrying, but they don't know what will tell them to *go ahead* with marriage. And though they enter the relationship saying that marriage is only a *possibility*—they "aren't sure" if they should marry—they have only one exit plan: to marry. They've never made provision for the possibility that they won't marry. All in all, they have a very mushy idea of how the relationship will end: how they will know if they should or should not proceed toward marriage, and what they will do if they decide marriage is not the way they should go.

Whether the lack of definition is in the middle of a relationship or at the end, undefined commitments are dangerous.

Grahame and Janine, for instance, were dating each other "seriously." They had committed themselves to find out whether they ought to get married. After about nine months, Grahame proposed to Janine that they should, indeed, get married. At the time, however, Janine was struggling with a couple of character traits in Grahame that drove her crazy. She wasn't sure she wanted to marry him.

Grahame and Janine didn't move toward marriage, but they did continue to go out.

Six months later, Janine finally decided that she and Grahame were a good match. By that point, however, Grahame was no longer so confident. The fact that Janine had taken six months to make her decision bothered him. Could she really love him if it took her so long to decide?

Both of them were frustrated in their relationship, but they decided they'd invested too much in one another to quit going together, so they continued to go out. Four months later, Grahame decided that, sure enough, Janine did love him and he'd been a fool not to recognize it. Now, however, when he brought it up, Janine was waffling.

After more than three years of bouncing back and forth, more than a dozen sessions of psychological counseling, and after months of feeling guilty—first, for having held up Grahame by failing to be ready for marriage when he had first been ready and later, for thinking of actually calling the relationship off—Janine finally decided it was time to put a halt to their relationship. Guilty or not, she figured, she had to get out. She wasn't convinced she and Grahame should *not* marry; in fact, she thought, maybe one day they would marry. But for right then, it was "no good for us to keep going."

Grahame and Janine broke up.

Grahame confessed later that secretly he'd been relieved when the break had come. "I knew it [the relationship] was doing neither of us any good. But I didn't want to be the one to put a stop to it."

Brian and Carol faced a similar frustration. Brian asked Carol to commit herself to him so they could pursue the possibility of marriage. She did. Five months later, however, Carol received a job transfer to Chicago. Brian wasn't ready yet to ask Carol to marry him, but since he didn't have anyone else in mind, he wasn't about to call off the relationship, either. Carol felt she was in a bind. "Must I refuse to date other guys?" she asked. "What am I supposed to do when I get to Chicago? Stay home and wait for Brian to call? What if I become attracted to a guy in Chicago? And what if Brian falls in love with someone else here?"

Carol was upset that Brian was unwilling to make a bigger commitment, and Brian felt his trust was betrayed when Carol told him she wanted to break up. Brian and Carol had enjoyed a warm and loving friendship before they'd become "serious." Now they could barely speak to one another.

Lionel Haines, a venture capitalist who has helped start at least five businesses, counsels entrepreneurs who are just beginning: "Never launch a business without an exit plan."[2] The same advice is appropriate in all human relationships: Never enter a relationship without an exit plan.

Of course when you start a company, you do so with the idea of staying in business forever. But, says Haines, even though you plan to remain in business for the rest of your life, you must *always have an exit plan.*

When you enter into an agreement, whether to buy a loaf of bread or to pursue marriage, the terms of the agreement—"the price and the time period . . . and the terms of a buyout"—should be clear from the start.

You buy a loaf of bread in a day-old store. When you bring it home, you discover it's so stale you can't eat it. "Sorry!" says the storekeeper when you bring it back for exchange. "You bought it; you eat it—or you throw it away. The signs clearly state our store policy: No Returns."

You buy a loaf of bread from your local grocery store. You don't like the way it tastes. "Bring it back!" says the manager. "We say 'Satisfaction Guaranteed,' and we mean it."

You marry. You don't like the man you've married. "Sorry!" says the Lord. "You married him. You committed yourself to him 'for better, for worse, for richer, for poorer, in sickness and in health . . . till death do [you] part.' There's no backing out. You knew the 'terms of sale' when you married him. There is no exit plan in marriage. No honorable exit, anyway. Not before death. If you want to exit your marriage before either one of you dies, then you'll have to break your vows. But you know what I say about that!"

So now you're proposing to your sister that the two of you start "going" together or that you should "pursue the possibility of marriage." What are the terms of the agreement? And what's the exit plan? Do you have those things nailed down?

Brothers and sisters don't leave room for mistakes—vows that may need to be broken, promises that may never be fulfilled. Brothers and sisters define the terms of their relationships and don't make commitments without an exit plan.

Guilty or Not Guilty?

I have tried to write the stories of Tracy and Grant, Grahame and Janine, and Brian and Carol so as to give both parties in each case an equal claim to justice.

Who muffed up in Grant's and Tracy's relationship? He said he wanted to be "just friends." Do friends walk hand-in-hand? Do they kiss each other good-night? Do they hug and kiss and fondle the way Grant and Tracy eventually did? I fault Grant more than I do Tracy. He should have been more honest with himself. But Tracy, too, could have stopped the miscommunication. The moment Grant first put his arm around her, she could have said, "Uh-h-h, Grant? I thought we were going to be 'just friends.' I don't think 'just friends' do this kind of thing." It would have cleared the air real fast—no assumptions, no implications and inferences. Tracy would have heard explicit communication: "Oh. Yeah. I guess I did say we were going to be just friends, didn't I?" (Right.) "And I guess you're right. Friends don't hold each other like this, do they?" (Right again.) "Sorry about that." Or else Grant would have said, "Yeah, I did say that, but I'm starting to think I'd rather have you as my girlfriend." And Tracy could have responded to him from that base.

But Tracy didn't question Grant's motives. She didn't seek clarification. And so she got burned. And he thought he was innocent. Or at least he pretended to think he was innocent.

And what about Grahame and Janine and Brian and Carol? Did they need to do what they did: enter a commitment in which an exit plan was undefined? Of course not! They could have stated right at the start: "I am willing to commit myself to date only you for a period of three months" (or six or nine months—or whatever term they were willing to obligate themselves). But they had no reason to make the open-ended commitments they did. (Indeed, as we'll find in chapter 6, brothers and sisters don't enter into exclusive dating agreements or any kinds of commitments to pursue the possibility of marriage. They have no need to.)

Brothers and sisters know that physical actions communicate; therefore, they do all in their power to make their physical actions correspond with their verbal affirmations. Brothers and sisters also know that if they do not clearly define what they mean when they make a commitment, they are likely to find themselves obligated for things they don't intend. Therefore, they refuse to make commitments without explicitly stating what they have in mind and without agreeing to an exit plan.

Questions for Study and Discussion

1. Do you think it is true that men and women communicate by their actions as much as they do by their words? What evidence do you have for your conclusion?

2. If you think people communicate by their actions, do you think they should be held accountable for what they say in this manner? Why or why not?

3. Should a person be held accountable for implying a commitment to do something if he never makes a specific promise in that regard? Why or why not? How does Jesus' command in Matthew 5:37 relate to this question?

4. If someone misinterprets another person's intent based on that person's actions, who should be held accountable for the misunderstanding, and under what circumstances?

5. Is it possible to promise something and not be aware you're making the promise? If so, can you think of examples where you or someone you know has done this? If not, how do you interpret Leviticus 5:4 where God says, "If a person . . . takes an oath to do anything, whether good or evil . . . even though he is unaware of it, in any case when he learns of it he will be guilty"?

6. Suppose one of your friends implied in every way possible (but didn't use words to directly say) that he was committed to doing something or going somewhere with you. Then, at the last minute, just before the event was supposed to happen, he said, "Hey! I never said I'd do that!" How would you feel? Would that experience help build or destroy your trust in your friend?

7. What if you had experiences like the one described in question 6 several times over with the same person: you were convinced he was going to do something, and then he said, "I understand why you'd think that, but I never said I was committed. . . ." How would you feel? What would that do to your trust in that person?

8. How could you reduce the chances of having your actions misinterpreted?

9. How could Tracy have protected herself against Grant's deceptive physical communication?

10. Jim Talley and Bobbie Reed suggest that when a man and woman want to get to know each other better, they should enter into a formal relational agreement: "The first step in taking responsibility for the relationship is for the couple to sit down, discuss, and agree upon the limits for the relationship. Next, they need to review their agreement with their pastor or a spiritual leader in the church and make a commitment to live within the agreement."[3] They say that the couple should write out the agreement and that they and their spiritual leader should all sign the agreement. Further, the couple should be held accountable to the agreement by the spiritual authority.

Talley and Reed have a sample agreement upon which one might wish to base one's own agreement. In the sample, they suggest, "This agreement will cover a period of _____ months, from _____ to _____."[4]

a. Comment on the idea of entering into a formal, written relational agreement. What advantages do you see for such a thing? What disadvantages?

b. If you were to write an agreement, to what would you be willing to obligate yourself? To what would you *want* to be obligated?

c. Comment on the idea of using a defined time period as an exit plan for a relational agreement. What are the advantages and disadvantages of using such a scheme? What other strategies could you use as exit plans?

d. Comment on the idea of being held accountable to a relational agreement by a spiritual authority. Could such an arrangement be helpful? Is such an arrangement necessary? Why or why not?

e. Do regular friends ever enter into formal relational agreements? If so, under what circumstances? If not, why not?

f. Is there a reason why brothers and sisters should enter into formal relational agreements? Why or why not?

g. If you were to enter into a formal relational agreement, what kind of exit plan would you want?

11. Often when a man or woman wants to break up with a dating partner, he or she will feel guilty about the prospect. As expressed in the Introduction: "Staying together is . . . perceived as honorable, while breaking up is not."

a. In your opinion, are these feelings legitimate? Are they based in reality? Or should people really have no feelings of guilt, honor, or dishonor when it comes to the matter of breaking up?

b. If there is no legitimate basis for these feelings, where do they come from? Why do so many people have them?

c. If there is a legitimate basis for these feelings, what is it?

12. Having read this chapter, look again at your answers to question 1.c. in the Introduction. Was/is your answer complete? Do vows have anything to do with the beginning of a boyfriend-girlfriend or "serious" dating relationship?

a. If boyfriend-girlfriend and "serious" dating relationships *are* based on vows, are those vows legitimate? Are they something God approves of? Why or why not? Is "breaking up" legitimate? Is it something God condones? Why or why not?

b. If boyfriend-girlfriend and "serious" dating relationships are *not* based on vows, then continue with your explanations from question 11: why do we see the rest of the phenomena described in the Introduction? Why the sense of obligation to keep going? Why the sudden start and stop to such relationships? Why the pain of breaking up? Are you able to explain adequately all these phenomena?

He who guards his lips guards his soul, but he who speaks rashly will come to ruin.

Proverbs 13:3

Do to others as you would have them do to you.

Luke 6:31

5

WHITE LIES AND PROMISES

Brothers and Sisters Differentiate Between Romantic Interest, Commitments, and Obligations

J eff is a friend of mine. He's thirteen and just launching out into the realm of dating. This past Valentine's Day he asked me what I thought of his idea of giving a large candy heart to Wendy, a girl in his class whom he likes.

"Would you want to give a heart like that to anyone else in your class?" I asked.

"No," he replied. "I couldn't afford it! They're three bucks apiece!"

"Then giving Wendy a candy heart will kind of put her in a special category, won't it?"

"Yeah. I guess so."

Jeff and I discussed how he could show more equal concern for all the members of his class. We came up with the idea of having him give chocolate kisses to everyone.

Some time later, when I told Dale about my conversation with Jeff, Dale became hostile and dramatic. He slammed his hand into his chest, snapped his head back, scrunched his eyes, and grunted—"Unhhh!"—as if he'd been shot. Then he said loudly: "You've got to be kidding! I can't believe you! What possible reason is there that Jeff should hide his feelings toward Wendy? You say the candy heart would put Wendy in a special category. She already *is* in a special category! He *likes* her more than he does everyone else in his class. Why should he hide those feelings behind a mask of 'equal concern'?" He paused briefly, then added, "Y'know, you talk about being honest and consistent and walking with integrity. I think you're telling Jeff to be *dis*honest! It's certainly less honest for him to give chocolate kisses to everyone in his class than it would be for him to give Wendy a candy heart."

"Suppose Jeff were twenty-seven and already married," I responded. "Would you feel differently about my counsel? Suppose Jeff had the same special feelings for Wendy but was already married to Chris. Do you think he should give Wendy a candy heart?"

"Of course not!" Dale replied. "But you said he is only thirteen. And he *isn't* married yet!"

Dale's response intrigued me. In our culture people seem to think that when you're not married it's not only acceptable but actually mandatory that you tell people to whom you're attracted that you have those special feelings. As long as it's true, that's all that matters. After you're married, of course, the issue of honesty is less important than whether you're true to your marriage vows.

I think Dale's attitude toward marriage vows is correct. Once you're married you should limit your expressions of romantic love to only one person—your husband or wife. But we must judge our speech by far more than our marital status and the bald truthfulness of what we want to communicate.

Just because I have a romantic interest in you doesn't mean I've myself committed to you. And even if I'm committed to get to know you, it doesn't mean I have to tell you I'm committed.

White Lies

Cal and Bobbi were friends; they'd been friends for several years. Bobbi had been romantically attracted to Cal for most of that time, but Cal had never reciprocated until the day he "fell in love" with Bobbi and began expressing his feelings to her.

Over the course of the next few weeks, Cal expressed his romantic interest several times. Then one night a couple of months later he said, "Bobbi, what do you think of the idea of us getting married?"

She paused momentarily before answering to see if he was serious. There was a yearning in his eyes and a faint smile on his lips. "I'm ready!" She beamed.

"Well," he said, "when would you want the wedding to be?" They talked about dates. July tenth seemed reasonable. With that settled, Cal said, "Got any ideas who you'd want for bridesmaids?"

By the time they parted later that night, Bobbi's head was spinning. The wedding was going to be July 10. Julie and Trish, Sally and Denise were going to be bridesmaids. She and Cal were going to go shopping for a ring.

A couple of nights later they went to a movie. Afterward they went out for cake and coffee. "Cal," said Bobbi as they sat waiting for their dessert to arrive, "unhh . . . I hate to put pressure on you, but, y'know, if we're going to get married July tenth, I've got a lot of work to do and. . . ."

"Huh?" he looked surprised. "Oh! You're talking about the other night, huh?" Bobbi blanched as she sensed Cal was about to tell her something she didn't want to hear. "Uh-h-h, yeah," Cal said. "I got to thinking later that you might have taken it the wrong way." He spoke slowly, as if he were weighing every word. "Y'know, when I said what I did, I wasn't asking you to marry me."

"*What?*" Bobbi exploded. The force with which she expressed it caused a few of the other patrons in the restaurant to look in their direction. She tried to restrain herself but succeeded poorly. "You weren't asking me to marry you! What *were* you doing?

You asked me if I wanted to marry you! I have told my parents . . . !"

"Oh, Bobbi!" Cal's voice was taut. "I didn't . . . Oh . . . !" He looked down and shook his head. "All I was trying to do was find out what you thought of the idea, how you *felt* about it, what kinds of thinking you'd been doing. I'm not ready to marry you! Maybe in another year. . . . I mean, I *want* to marry you, but . . ."

Bobbi was furious. "So why'd you have to bring up the stupid subject?" She threw down her napkin, grabbed her purse, and dashed from their table. She wanted to go—anywhere but to be near this man who'd deceived her. And Cal *had* deceived her! He'd betrayed her trust! She couldn't believe it.

Cal was correct; he hadn't said, "I'm committing myself to marry you." But then, how many future husbands propose marriage with the words, "I hereby commit myself to marry you?" Most men simply ask, "Will you marry me?" That's basically what Cal had done, isn't it? With his initial question and all the other things he and Bobbi had talked about that night, it was the communicative equivalent of holding out a ring to her and saying, "Will you marry me?" Bobbi had said yes. And then when she reached out to accept the ring, Cal pulled it back and snarled, "I didn't say I would marry you!"

Do You Know What You're Saying?

When talking about marriage or, for that matter, about any type of committed relationship, what matters is *commitment*, not thoughts, not feelings. Who cares if you have some thoughts? Who cares if you experience feelings? Anyone can have thoughts and anyone can experience feelings. What Wendy and Bobbi (and, I hope, Jeff and Cal) want to know—what they should *demand* to know—is: is there *commitment*? *Commitment* is what hangs on when feelings change (as feelings always will).

Jeff, happily, recognized he doesn't have control over his emotions. He can control how he *acts* as a result of his emotions, but his emotions simply "are." They exist; they come and go. And so what if he happens to like Wendy? The question he and every one of us needs to answer is not, Do I have feelings for this other person? Rather, the question we need to answer is: Am I ready, willing, and able to place myself in a position of obligation to this particular brother or sister?

The moment I tell you I'm committed to you, I put myself in a position of obligation. Before I tell you of my commitment, it is my free choice whether I keep the commitment or not. If I'm committed to you but haven't told you about it, it doesn't matter if one day I decide I would rather "be there" for someone else. I have no more obligation to you than to any of my other brothers and sisters. I can be your special friend if I want to or I can be someone else's special friend. It's my choice. But once I tell you I'm committed to you, I am under obligation to fulfill my commitment, whether I want to be obligated in that way or not. That was the point of the previous chapter: when brothers and sisters make promises, they fulfill them. God hates the lying tongue! If I tell you I'm committed to you and then fail to fulfill that commitment, I have lied to you and placed myself under the condemnation of God.

Jeff wanted to tell Wendy the truth: "I like you." But if he had told her, he would have misled her by focusing on truth that was irrelevant to issues of real importance. He would, if you will, have told her a *white lie*. Not even Jeff was terribly concerned whether Wendy understood his feelings. Permeating his idea of giving Wendy a candy heart was his desire to tell her he was committed to her.

Imagine if he had given Wendy the candy heart and she'd responded, "Oh, thanks, Jeff! That was really sweet of you!"—the kind of response she might give a friend: "You're a good friend. I like you." Would Jeff be satisfied? I think not.

Suppose he had come right out and said, "Wendy, I like you," and she had responded, "Oh, that's nice, Jeff! I like you, too." Would he be satisfied with that response? No, not with that response either.

"No, no, no, Wendy," he would probably say. "You don't understand. I don't just 'like' you. I *like* you."

"Oh-h-h-h!" she would say, catching his drift. Suddenly that warm, glowing feeling would start rising in Jeff's chest. "Well I like you, too, Jeff," she would say. "I mean, I really, really like you. Better than anyone else."

Ahh! Suddenly Jeff beams with a smile that can't be wiped off his face. And Wendy beams, too. They start declaring their love and commitment: "We're 'going' together." "We belong to one another." "We're committed." And Jeff and Wendy's relationship isn't just friends anymore.

Now the crucial question: Was it some statement on Jeff's part about having a positive regard for Wendy that brought about these changes? I think not! As he said, "I don't just 'like' you. I *like* you." Put another way: I'm committed to you.

"Are you?" I asked him. "Are you committed to her? Are you willing to be obligated to her in the matter? If so, to what are you willing to obligate yourself?"

The truth was, he couldn't answer. He didn't know if he was really committed to Wendy. And he was unable to say to what he was willing to be obligated. I told him it was better to keep his mouth shut and give everyone in his class a chocolate kiss: "Wait until you're ready before you make commitments."

Cal faced a situation almost identical to Jeff's. He told Bobbi the truth: "I feel like marrying you," but he focused on truth that was irrelevant—something that should have been irrelevant, anyway—to both him and Bobbi as they considered the prospects of marrying each other.

It should have made no difference that he was experiencing some positive emotions toward Bobbi. And it should have made no difference that she happened to have some emotional tugs toward him. Emotions can't provide a solid foundation for marriage. Our emotions change every minute of the day. The big question Cal and Bobbi had to answer concerning marriage was not, Do I have feelings for you? but, Am I willing to commit myself to you?

By asking an irrelevant question, Cal misled Bobbi. He distracted her from a far more important question: Are we willing to commit ourselves one to the other for the rest of our lives?

Jesus said, "Do to others as you would have them do to you" (Luke 6:31). Most of us believe, I think, that friends are people we can trust to tell us the truth *no matter what the cost.* It is certainly the case that these are the kinds of friends we would *prefer* to have. We would prefer that our friends tell us the truth rather than hide it behind white lies and irrelevant remarks.

Brothers and sisters do everything in their power to avoid leading each other on, misleading each other, or distracting each other from those matters that are of greatest significance. They do this by refusing to send each other insignificant or irrelevant messages. And when one person focuses on emotions and ignores the matter of commitment, the other makes sure to raise the question: "I'm glad you have those emotions. I have emotions. I have emotions like that as well. But what difference should our emotions make in our relationship?"

Some Rules of Tongue

Two weeks before Sarita and I were engaged, I was at my parents' home. I went out on a date with Carrie, the girl who had been my first girlfriend in high school. Carrie and I had a good time that night. So good, in fact, that the next morning I told Sally, a mutual friend of ours, "I wouldn't be surprised if Carrie and I get married."

It was the result of the very mistake I have just described: I failed to distinguish my emotional state from my state of commitment. While, in a way, my comment was truthful, saying those words was one of the stupidest things I have ever done! First, the comment itself was wrong-headed. I should have been wise enough to know that just because Carrie and I had enjoyed a nice evening together and just because I was experiencing the emotions I was experiencing didn't mean I had a good basis for thinking Carrie and I might marry one day. More than that, however, I simply had no business talking about my feelings with Carrie or Sally.

In 2 Corinthians 10:5, Paul said he wanted to "take captive every thought to make it obedient to Christ." I'm sure my comments to Sally didn't help Carrie to "take captive every thought," especially not once she found out three weeks later that Sarita and I were engaged. I should have paid attention to this rule of tongue.

> *Rule of Tongue 1:* Whatever I say should help my brothers and sisters obey God. It should certainly not hinder them from obeying God!

In 1 Thessalonians 4:6, Paul tells the Thessalonians not to "wrong" or "take advantage" of their brothers and sisters. One of the ways in which men and women commonly wrong each other is by illegitimately raising each other's expectations for marriage.

What Cal did with Bobbi, I did with Carrie. When I talked about the possibility of our getting married, I preyed upon Carrie's emotions. By saying what I did, I wronged Carrie and, in a way, Sally, too, by illegitimately raising their expectations and leading them to believe I would do something I was not then nor ever would be prepared to do.

> *Rule of Tongue 2:* Whatever I say, I must refrain from leading my brothers and sisters to believe I will do something that I am not now nor possibly ever will be ready, willing, or able to do.

Ephesians 4:29 says, "Do not let any unwholesome talk come out of your mouths, but only what is helpful for building others up according to their needs, that it may benefit those who listen."

What I told Sally didn't help build Carrie up. It didn't build up Sally, either. Nor did it meet their needs. Finally, it was of no benefit to either Carrie or Sally.

Now, I may try to excuse myself by saying that no one can always and only say things that build others up, meet their needs, and benefit them. But while it is true that I would have a difficult time proving everything I say has a positive benefit to those who listen, I would have no difficulty demonstrating that my words were *un*helpful to Sally and Carrie.

Had I never said the things I did, I'm sure Carrie and Sally both would have been far happier than they were three weeks later when they discovered I was engaged to someone else! What I said may have tickled Sally's and Carrie's imaginations, but it was neither helpful, necessary, nor beneficial. I built no one up through my comments, and once they discovered that Sarita and I were engaged, it turned out that my comments *did* tear a couple of someones down.

Rule of Tongue 3: My communication with my brothers and sisters must be helpful, necessary, beneficial. At least it must not be unhelpful or unbeneficial.

The problem I had, the problem Jeff faced, the problem Cal and Bobbi and every one of us faces is not that we have emotions. We all have emotions; they're part of who we are as human beings. The problem we must address is how we will control our tongues. Who or what will rule: God or our emotions? "Set a guard over my mouth, O LORD; keep watch over the door of my lips," wrote David (Psalm 141:3).

I knew when I spoke to Sally that I wasn't prepared to make a marriage commitment to Carrie. I didn't know that I would *never* be prepared. I ardently desired that one day I would be. In fact, I had harbored an on-again-off-again hope that Carrie and I would be married ever since we first started "going" together in tenth grade. But whether I was eventually to marry Carrie or not, the fact that at the time I talked to Sally I wasn't prepared to make a commitment in that regard should have made me hold my tongue.

In essence, what got me in trouble was not that I was honest about my feelings, but that I was not honest enough about everything else that's related to getting married: all the things that make a marriage work. If I had been truly honest I would not have said, "I wouldn't be surprised if Carrie and I get married." Nor would I have said, "The way I feel right now, I wouldn't be surprised. . . ." Both of those statements, like white lies, would have been true but irrelevant.

If I had felt compelled to say something (and I'm convinced I should have felt no such compulsion), what I should have said is something like, "Boy! Carrie and I sure did have a good time last night!" It would have been true and would have expressed everything that needed to be said.

Guard Your Heart

Being transparent, open, and honest in our dealings with one another did not mean that my sisters and I could speak without restraint on any matters we happened to choose. Even after we were engaged, I refused to tell Sarita the intimate details of how I sometimes responded to the touch of her hand. She wanted to know why I felt obliged to quit holding her hand at various points. "I'm sorry," I would say, "I'm just becoming too stimulated sexually."

She wanted to know more about what that meant. "You'll have to wait until we're married," I said. Some things are best left unsaid.

In Proverbs, we read:

> Above all else, guard your heart, for it is the wellspring of life. Put away perversity from your mouth; keep corrupt talk far from your lips. Let your eyes look straight ahead, fix your gaze directly before you. Make level paths for your feet and take only ways that are firm. Do not swerve to the right or the left; keep your foot from evil.
>
> My son, pay attention to my wisdom, listen well to my words of insight, that you may maintain discretion and your lips may preserve knowledge. For the lips of an adulteress drip honey, and her speech is smoother than oil; but in the end she is bitter as gall, sharp as a double-edged sword. Her feet go down to death; her steps lead straight to the grave. . . .

Now then, my sons, listen to me; do not turn aside from what I say. Keep to a path far from her, do not go near the door of her house, lest you give your best strength to others and your years to one who is cruel, lest strangers feast on your wealth and your toil enrich another man's house. . . .

Drink water from your own cistern, running water from your own well. Should your springs overflow in the streets, your streams of water in the public squares? Let them be yours alone, never to be shared with strangers. May your fountain be blessed, and may you rejoice in the wife of your youth. (4:23—5:5; 5:7–10, 15–18)

That married man is a fool who would tell a woman to whom he is not married, "Every time I see you, I go weak inside. I'm crazy with desire for you." And that woman is a fool who would be swayed by such foolish speech on the part of a married man.

What is the warning God gave us? For a man: Be careful of the wayward woman. For a woman: Be careful of the wayward man. Guard your heart. Guard your steps. Don't go near the place where you are likely to be tempted, whether to sin or to behave foolishly.

What is true for married men and women is equally valid for those who are not yet married. You have no business talking about your wayward desires to the woman or man toward whom your desire is pulling you! "Should your springs overflow in the streets, your streams of water in the public squares? Let them be yours alone, never to be shared with strangers" (Proverbs 5:16–17).

If you know and trust your brother or sister well enough to give your heart away, then fine: give it away, make a marriage vow. But if you're not able or willing to entrust the rest of your life to this other person, *hold your tongue, guard your heart!* "Above all else, guard your heart, for it is the wellspring of life" (Proverbs 4:23). Give your heart away to the wrong people and they will use it against you.

Solomon wrote,

My son, if you have put up security for your neighbor, if you have struck hands in pledge for another, if you have been trapped by what you said, ensnared by the words of your mouth, then do this, my son, to free yourself, since you have fallen into your neighbor's hands: Go and humble yourself; press your plea with your neighbor! Allow no sleep to your eyes, no slumber to your eyelids. Free yourself, like a gazelle from the hand of the hunter, like a bird from the snare of the fowler. (Proverbs 6:1–5)

Better to avoid the trap in the first place than to have to extricate yourself later.

Brothers and sisters guard their hearts. They distinguish between romantic interest, commitment, and obligation. And they refuse to make unspoken, unintentional, unwanted, or unmeant promises. They say what they mean and mean what they say. Brothers and sisters are honest.

Questions for Study and Discussion

1. What is the difference between *promising* you'll do something, *implying* you'll do it, and simply *being committed* to doing it?

2. Is there anything wrong with being committed to someone without making a promise or vow? How about the other way around: is there anything wrong with making a promise or vow and not being committed to fulfilling it?

3. If you have a feeling toward someone, are you obligated to tell them about it? How about if you're committed to them: do you have to tell them about your commitment? Why or why not? What are some reasons you may or may not want to tell another person about your feelings or commitments?

4. Suppose Jeff had given Wendy the candy heart. In what ways would he have been obligated to Wendy?

   a. Would he be free to give similar candy hearts to other girls in his class?

b. Why or why not?

5. How would you have counseled Jeff if he had asked you about giving a candy heart to the girl of his dreams?

6. What advice would you give Cal and Bobbi?

7. In this chapter we are urged to guard our hearts: "Give your heart away to the wrong person and you'll lose your life; he or she will use it against you."

    a. Have you ever seen someone use someone else's emotional commitment against them: to hold the other person under obligation, for instance, or to punish the other person in some way or another? Describe the situation.

    b. How could a premature commitment (i.e., giving your heart away too soon) be used against you?

8. Do traditional wedding vows require a couple to make commitments with respect to their emotions? If so, what kinds of commitments do they make? If not, why do you think they are not required to make such commitments?

9. In your opinion, what do you think motivates people to obligate themselves to one another when they aren't yet sure they can or want to make a commitment? What benefits do they think they will receive from premature obligation?

9. Summarize the message of this chapter.

Do you not know that your body is a temple of the Holy Spirit, who is in you, whom you have received from God? You are not your own; you were bought at a price. Therefore honor God with your body.

1 Corinthians 6:19–20

Christ's love compels us, because we are convinced that one died for all, and therefore all died. And he died for all, that those who live should no longer live for themselves but for him who died for them and was raised again.

2 Corinthians 5:14–15

6

WHO'S PULLING THE STRINGS?

Brothers and Sisters Refuse to Obligate Themselves One to Another

Gary was romantically interested in Jean, so he began asking her out and paying her way to dinners, movies, games, a concert. Gary seemed happy enough with the arrangement and Jean, too, was satisfied until, at the end of their thirteenth date, Gary dropped her off at her door. As they lingered a moment on the doorstep, Gary looked at Jean imploringly for the smallest fraction of a second. Suddenly he turned away from her and stormed off. Later he explained that he had become angry when he realized Jean wasn't going to give him a good-night kiss. Not that she had ever done so before. She'd never even held his hand! But standing there on her doorstep, he said, it suddenly all crashed in on him: he felt as if she'd been taking advantage of him, using him as a ticket to free entertainment.

Paula had similar feelings when a man she met at work one day asked if she would like to go to a concert. She was delighted by the idea. She didn't know much about her host except that he was one of her company's better customers and seemed like a nice guy. That night he picked her up from her apartment in a chauffeur-driven limousine. He then took her out to an eighty-dollar-a-plate restaurant. That was *before* the concert.

"I should have guessed what was coming," she told me. "After the concert he invites me up to his place. He wants to have sex. I tell him I'm not interested. He's upset. He says: 'After all I've done for you?'"

Question: did Jean take advantage of Gary? Because he'd taken her out, was Jean under obligation to hold Gary's hand or to kiss him good-night? How about Paula? Paula said she felt as if her host tried to take advantage of her. On the other hand, he seemed to believe she had taken advantage of him: "After all I've done for you?!" Did Paula take advantage of her host? Who had what kinds of obligations to whom?

Dates, time spent together, gifts . . . any or all of these things can create a sense of obligation in the mind of the one who is giving the gift as much as in the heart of the one receiving it. No one may even have that purpose on their mind. They know the gift should create no sense of obligation. But the feelings come, nevertheless. I know women who have felt obliged to marry men because they accepted gifts from them—cameras, expensive sewing machines, cars, beautiful coats. The more expensive the gift, the more obligated they seemed to feel. "How can I say no to a guy who has given me such (a) wonderful gift(s)?" they ask.

Brothers and sisters seek to avoid these kinds of situations. They do everything in their power to avoid obligating themselves to one another.

Brothers and Sisters Claim No Ownership Rights

Phil and Donna were co-workers and had been friends and occasional dating partners for several months. Phil's feelings toward Donna started to grip him powerfully, so one day he said, "Donna, I'm really interested in you. I don't know if we ought to get married, but I'd like us to pursue that possibility. I'm wondering what you would think if we entered into an agreement not to date anyone else and to really concentrate on our own relationship—and see how things go?"

It turned out that Donna's interest in Phil was as strong as his in her, so they made the agreement. Some time later, Phil came to speak to me. "I've heard you probably wouldn't like the kind of relationship Donna and I have," he said. "If that's true, I'd like to know why."

"You've heard correctly," I responded. I told him of my objections to indefinite promises with nonexistent exit plans (see chapter 4). "I also object to the whole idea of ownership, and I object to it for several reasons. One is Scriptural. The others are more practically based."

I started with the Scriptural objection.

Who Rightfully Owns You?

When one person gives another the right to dictate who he will spend time with, what he will do, or where or why he will do what he does, he has given that person the right of an owner. "It seems to me you and Donna have entered into a mutual ownership relationship," I said to Phil. "You own Donna and Donna owns you. You have obligated yourself to Donna not to spend time with other sisters unless and until she lets you. And Donna has obligated herself to you in the same way. More or less, the two of you have placed yourselves under each other's control. The question is, has God given either of you the right to place yourselves under one another's control? I believe not."

In Scripture, there are several relationships in which God recognizes one person's right to own another. For instance,

God, as Creator, has the primary right of ownership over everything He has made and supreme right over everything He has redeemed. "Do you not know that your body is a temple of the Holy Spirit, who is in you, whom you have received from God? You are not your own; you were bought at a price," God tells us in 1 Corinthians 6:19–20. As a result of His purchasing us from sin and death, He says He owns us; we have a responsibility to honor Him with our bodies.

"Christ's love compels us, because we are convinced that [he] died for all, and therefore all died. And he died for all, that those who live should no longer live for themselves but for him who died for them and was raised again" (2 Corinthians 5:14–15).

God has purchased you; He has the right of an owner over you. If you refuse to allow God to exert His rights as your owner, then Satan will control you (see Matthew 6:24; Galatians 5:2–6, 16–18; Ephesians 2:1–7; Colossians 1:13; 1 John 5:19). If you're a Christian, however, you have committed yourself to giving God what is His by right. In other words, you've committed yourself to living as one who is owned by God.

Another ownership relationship ordained by God is that of parents with respect to their children.

Parents have subsidiary rights as owners of their children. " Sons are a heritage from the LORD," says Psalm 127:3, "children a reward from him."

Then there is the ownership relation between husbands and wives.

Husbands and wives own each other. Indeed, of the relationships I've mentioned, marriage is unique because in it there is mutual ownership. The Bible clearly states that "the wife's body does not belong to her alone but also to her husband. In the same way, the husband's body does not belong to him alone but also to his wife" (1 Corinthians 7:4).

Brothers and sisters, however, are given no right to place themselves under one another's ownership. They are commanded to submit to one another and to love one another (see Ephesians 5:21; John 13:34). They are commanded to serve each other and consider others better than themselves (see Matthew 20:25–28; Galatians 5:13; Philippians 2:3–4). But brothers and sisters are never given the right to command each other or to allow others to command them.

"In your relationship with Donna," I said to Phil, "you and Donna have given each other rights—the rights of owners. You've said to each other, 'You have the right to tell me who I may or may not spend time with. You have the right to limit what I do and with whom I do it.' The problem I have with that arrangement is that *God hasn't given you the right to give each other those privileges.*"

If the lack of a specific command were all I had, I would probably keep my mouth shut. We face hundreds of opportunities every day that the Bible doesn't specifically address. That doesn't mean we ought to avoid them. So I told Phil there were practical reasons, too, why I believe ownership relations between brothers and sisters are wrong.

Brothers and Sisters Refuse to Limit Social Contacts

In real estate, when one person, Mr. Gray, wants to sell his house, he won't automatically pull his house off the market the moment another person, Mr. Johnson, says he's considering buying it. He recognizes the truth that just because someone shows *interest* in the house doesn't mean he's committed to buy it (see chapter 5). Johnson must give Gray some form of payment to make it worth Gray's while to pull the house off the market. Otherwise, Johnson may come back three weeks later and say, "Sorry, but I've decided to buy something else," and Gray could have lost the best opportunity he ever had to sell his house. A third party, Mr. Smith, may have come by during those three weeks and said he wanted to buy Gray's house. Smith even offered to pay Gray more than what Gray had been asking. But Gray turned down Smith's offer. Why? Because Gray had told Johnson he wouldn't allow anyone else to buy the house until Johnson had come to a decision.

So what happens if Johnson comes to a decision and it's negative? What has Gray gained by committing himself not to sell his house until Johnson comes to a decision? Nothing. What has he lost? The opportunity to sell his house for more than he was asking! By obligating himself to Johnson not to sell the house until Johnson comes to a decision, Gray gains nothing and loses a lot, *unless Johnson offers Gray adequate compensation for the risk.*

"What bothers me about the relationship you have with Donna, at least as you've described it," I said to Phil, "is that the two of you are playing Johnson and Gray with one another— Johnson and Gray *without compensation.* You're asking Donna to be Mr. Gray while you play Mr. Johnson. You're asking her to take herself out of what we might call the 'dating market' while you make a decision about whether or not you want to marry her. And Donna is playing Mr. Johnson to you while you agree to act like Mr. Gray to her. You're taking yourself out of the 'dating market,' too, while she comes to a decision concerning you.

"Yet while you've agreed to these terms, neither one of you has anything to gain from the obligations to which you've committed yourselves and both of you have a lot to lose."

"I think I'd have to disagree," said Phil. "I don't see that we're losing anything; and I *do* see we're gaining a lot: we're spending a lot of time together, time we wouldn't be able to spend together if we didn't have the commitment that we do."

I questioned him on that idea. "You say you're gaining because you have more time for each other. Do you have more time for each other because you've openly committed yourselves to one another (because you're *obligated*)? Or do you have more time with each other because you're *willing* to spend more time together?"

"I'm not sure I see the difference," he said.

"It's the difference between being *committed* to doing something and being *obligated* to do it. You and Donna have now promised to spend time with one another and only with one another. Before you made that promise you were spending time together. You *could* have spent as much time together then as you do now. You simply chose not to. But now you're *obligated* to spend time together.

"Before, your motivation for being together was internal; you could spend whatever amount of time you wanted with whomever you wanted. Now your motivation is at least partially external. You and Donna *have to* spend time together; you have no freedom to spend time with other people; you've both given your word—you've promised—that this is the way you will conduct your affairs.

"My hypothesis is, you and Donna *didn't* need to obligate yourselves to one another in order to find the time together you feel you need."

"You might be right," Phil admitted. "On the other hand, I'm not sure we would have been *willing* to spend as much time together as we are now if we hadn't made the commitment. Why should we spend twenty or thirty hours a week together if we might not marry?"

"Tell me," I said.

"Huh?"

"Why should you spend twenty or thirty hours a week together if you might not marry?"

"But we're not . . . !" He stopped in mid-sentence and sighed.

"I don't know how much time you and Donna are spending together," I said. "It really doesn't matter. However much it is, I hope neither one of you is justifying the expense on the premise that the other person is committed, or virtually committed, to marriage. Neither one of you has made such a commitment. I think possibly both of you are *assuming* that the other has made such a commitment, or has *almost* made such a commitment. But the fact is, neither one of you has made that kind of commitment. You haven't communicated such a commitment, and, I dare say, you haven't made that kind of commitment in your hearts. Both of you may *want* to make such a commitment. You may *desire* it. But neither one of you is prepared to commit yourself to marriage."

Phil stood silently.

"How about if we change the course of our discussion?" I suggested. "You've just admitted you're not *gaining* anything from obligating yourselves to stay out of the dating market. You're gaining nothing of value, anyway—nothing that legitimizes the agreement you've made." (Phil grimaced, not wanting to concede the point.) "What do you have to *lose* because of the commitments you've made to one another?"

He shrugged. "I can't think of anything."

"All right. Let me try to help you," I offered. "First: *both of you have lost the freedom to date other people*. Not that either one of you is chomping at the bit to do that right now. But one day it might be nice to have that freedom." I told him the stories of Grahame and Janine and Brian and Carol (see chapter 4). "What if you came to the point where you decided that maybe you really *do* want to date someone else? Not that you've decided to *marry* someone else. Not that you've decided *not* to marry each other. It's just that you're still unsure on that point and it's been six months, or two years, or both of you sense the need to take a break from one another for a while. Maybe you think a break from each other could help clarify whether or not you should marry.

"According to what you've told me, unless both of you agree that you are not supposed to marry one another, if either one of you decides to date someone else, you will be breaking your promise." I mentioned to him some of the Scriptures we discussed in chapter 4. "Breaking your word is a major moral failing. God condemns such a thing.

"So that's the first cost you and Donna have forced yourselves to pay by entering into this kind of agreement. You have opened yourselves to the possibility—and, from my observation, the *strong* possibility—that you will break your word.

"Second, *both of you are limiting the amount of blessing you can give other people and the amount of blessing other people can give to you*. You've obligated yourselves not to go out with anyone else. Therefore, even if one of you has a free evening, if the other is tied up, the one who is free will not go out. You're *obligated* not to go out. Therefore, by your agreement, the two of you have guaranteed that an evening that could have been profitably spent blessing another brother or sister will not be spent that way.

"I think that's a shame. And a sin. How many brothers and sisters are there who would love to spend some time with either one of you—brothers and sisters whom you could bless or who could bless you? But you'll never spend that time with them because you and Donna have entered into a pact not to date anyone besides yourselves.

"Finally, to use the real estate analogy to its fullest: from what I gather, you and Donna are both interested in the possibility of getting married. Neither one of you is fully convinced that the other is 'the one,' yet you've asked each other not to consider the possibility of marrying anyone else until you both agree that you're not meant for each other. Talk about being in the position of a Mr. Gray!

"Prior to the time you obligated yourselves to one another, you both had the freedom to accept or reject any marriage proposals that came your way. Either one of you could negotiate whatever kinds of deals you wanted with whomever you wanted. Now, however, you've limited yourselves. Until the two of you absolve each other from this commitment, you're under obligation to negotiate exclusively one with the other. That would be a great deal for you both if both of you were simply Mr. Johnsons. Then you'd have all the time you wanted to look over the competition, to check out their features and prices. But neither one of you simply plays the role of Mr. Johnson. Both of you are also Mr. Gray; both of you have placed yourselves in a terrible position for negotiation. While the person you're negotiating with is bound not to negotiate with anyone else (a potential benefit), *you are bound in the same way!* Though your trading partner has no freedom to negotiate with anyone else, you have no freedom either. That means, while you've limited your trading partner's options—a possible curse to your partner!—you've also limited your own options—a possible curse to you! It's possible, just possible, that while you're in the midst of this exclusive relationship with Donna, both of you could end up missing the very best opportunities for marriage either of you ever had.

"To put it bluntly," I said, "as long as you hold Donna to her commitment not to go out with other guys, and as long as she holds you to your commitment not to go out with other girls, the two of you will only be seeking benefits for yourselves. There's no benefit to Donna in limiting her contacts with other brothers.

There's certainly no benefit for her brothers. In the same way, there's no benefit for you in not dating other sisters. Nor is there a benefit for your sisters in your being obligated not to date them.

"So, by obligating yourselves to limit your contacts with other members of the body, rather than maximizing the blessing you and Donna can give each other, and rather than maximizing the blessing you can give and receive from other members of the body, you and Donna are failing to fulfill God's primary purpose for having you spend time together."

Brothers and Sisters Avoid Mutual Obligation

Nancy came to me with what seemed to be the perfect objection to the kind of perspective I shared with Phil. "I've been friends with Brad for over three years now," she said. "We've never made any commitments to one another. Our relationship has been very casual, nice and enjoyable. But that's the problem. I'm twenty-seven and I'm at the point where I realize if I'm ever going to get married, I need to do something. Either Brad makes a move in the direction of marriage, or I have to tell him good-bye. I've *got* to. If I keep spending all my time with him and he never asks me to marry him, then I'm throwing away my chances for possibly marrying someone else."

Therefore, she was saying, isn't it far better to have a committed, mutually obligated relationship in which it's clear that both parties are pursuing marriage than to have a free-flowing relationship in which no one knows what the other is thinking and in which no one is obligated to do or say anything to the other?

In her January/February 1986 "The Elisabeth Elliot Newsletter," Elisabeth Elliot appears to raise the same objection. She said she wished she could "shout from the housetops" the idea that "close association and friendship . . . between a man and a woman who cannot get married, or who do not intend ever to get married, or who should not think of marriage for some years to come, is . . . seriously wrong." She explained: "It does not require several years for a man and woman to ascertain whether they are suited to one another for marriage. If it is possible, it is, after a reasonable time [six months to a year], obligatory on the man to speak of getting married before long."

At first glance it seems that both of these women are describing problems inherent in brother-sister relationships. Certainly they're describing brother-sister relationships, aren't they? How else should we interpret a "close association and friendship between a man and a woman" or a "very casual, nice and enjoyable" relationship in which the participants have "never made any commitments to one another"?

I am convinced that, despite their descriptions, Nancy and Ms. Elliot are not describing brother-sister relationships. Rather, they are describing virtually the same kind of relationship as Phil and Donna had. Nancy never explicitly mentions an obligation in her relationship with Brad, but she feels it nonetheless. Ms. Elliot is a bit more transparent.

You see, in a true brother-sister relationship it is never "obligatory on the man to speak of getting married." And if Nancy had been conducting herself toward Brad as a true sister in the Lord, she never would have come to the point where she felt frustrated because Brad wasn't "mak[ing] a move in the direction of marriage."

Brothers and sisters realize that it is quite possible for a man and woman to enjoy a "close association and friendship" without necessarily being interested in "ascertain[ing] whether they are suited to one another for marriage." It is *possible* that they will enter a relationship for that purpose, but in opposition to what Ms. Elliot suggests, there is nothing "seriously wrong" with a brother-sister relationship just because the participants are not considering the possibility of marriage. Indeed, simple observation tells us that far more men and women enter relationships for the purpose of friendship than to pursue marriage. Biological brothers and sisters enjoy relationships in which marriage is not in view; there is no reason brothers and sisters in the Lord may not do so as well.

Further, as I hope I've demonstrated in chapters 4 and 5, when it comes to morals and ethics, it is far safer for brothers and sisters to *refrain* from speaking of romantic interests and marriage than it is for them to make these things known. If "after a reasonable time" a man is interested in marrying his sister, and if he knows he is ready and willing to commit himself to her, then he is morally free to indicate his interest. But though he is *free* to indicate his interest, he is under no moral or ethical *obligation* to do so.

If a man is interested in marrying his sister in the Lord yet fails to reveal his interest, all he is doing is opening himself to the possibility that one day he will chide himself for being a fool. If his sister decides to marry someone else, he may think, "Why didn't I tell her I wanted to marry her? I should have said something!"

I believe that, rather than objecting to relationships in which the man feels no obligation to speak of marriage, what Nancy and Ms. Elliot are describing and objecting to is the situation where a sister is interested in marrying her brother in the Lord, refuses to speak of her interest, and then complains because her brother doesn't bring up the subject either. When a sister acts in this fashion, she likewise opens herself to the possibility of one day chiding herself for being a fool.

I suggested to Nancy that brothers and sisters don't generally enter into or evaluate their relationships according to those relationships' potential for ending in marriage. People don't establish and maintain regular friendships based on the possibility of marriage. Brothers and sisters in the Lord don't usually do these things either.

Most friendships are valid whether marriage is in view or not. The quality of the relationship—how it blesses the participants and those around them—is the sole basis on which brothers and sisters should normally decide whether or not to continue spending time together.

"So," I said to Nancy, "if your relationship with Brad is wholesome and mutually edifying, then you should maintain it, whether you plan to get married or not. If your relationship with Brad is unwholesome or unedifying, then you ought to abandon it, . . . *especially* if either one of you has been considering marriage. Why would you want to marry someone in whose presence you find yourself cursed?"

"Yes, yes, yes!" said Nancy. "But how do I get married? Everything you say sounds great *in theory* and maybe for someone who has years to go before they're ready for marriage. But I have a very busy schedule. If one of my brothers and I are supposed to determine if we should get married, we need to spend *significant* amounts of time together. And I can't possibly afford that much time with more than one guy. So how, under your model, do I get the time I need?"

"Right," I said. "So let me come to the point. Have you told Brad of your interest? Have you asked him if he's interested in marrying you?"

"Are you kidding?" she asked in apparent shock. "I mean, I've hinted enough about my interest. Why would I spend all the time I do with him unless I was interested in the possibility of marrying him? But I haven't *proposed marriage* to him, if that's what you're asking."

"That's what I'm asking," I admitted.

She was flustered. "It's the *guy's* job to ask the girl if she wants to get married. That's not the girl's job!"

"It isn't?" I responded in mock surprise. Of course, culturally, Nancy is absolutely correct. The man is supposed to propose. But as I've noted elsewhere, what is culturally acceptable is not always the same thing as what is Biblically required. "Is Brad concerned about you two getting married?" I asked.

"I don't know," said Nancy. "That's why I'm frustrated!"

"In other words, you *are* concerned about marriage, right?"

"Of course. That's what I've been saying."

"So why should you wait for Brad to mention the subject? If you're the one who wants to get married; if you're the one who is ready for marriage; if you're the one who trusts Brad enough and believes the two of you are suited to each other for doing what God wants you to do with your lives: *why should you wait for him to initiate?*"

She hesitated.

"Look," I said. "Is Brad your brother?" I paused, waiting for her to reply. I wanted her to say it.

"Yes," she finally admitted.

"Okay. Are you his sister?"

"Yes."

"So if he's your brother and you're his sister, shouldn't he be concerned about your welfare and what concerns you?"

"I guess so."

"Not, 'I guess so.' *Absolutely!* That's the first principle of brother-sister relationships: that brothers and sisters seek to bless and love each other as Jesus blessed and loved them.

"It seems to me, Nancy, if you want to marry Brad, you should say, 'Brad, I want to get married. I'd like to marry you if you'd like to marry me.' At least then the subject would be out on the table so you can discuss it. You'd find out very fast what Brad is thinking, and you'd be able to plan and act accordingly."

Brothers and sisters care for each other and seek to bless each other. If Nancy has a concern about marriage, then she needs to make her concern known so Brad can respond appropriately. Maybe he'll be embarrassed. "Oh, wow!" he'll say. "I've wanted to propose to you for two years now, Nancy, but I've been afraid to ask. I figured you'd say no!" Or maybe: "Nancy, I wish I could say I was ready to marry you. I care for you deeply. I'd love to marry you. But I'm just not prepared to make that kind of commitment to you. Not now." And who knows why he may not be ready? The conversation that ensues should help to clarify Brad's personal insecurities and fears. Or perhaps Nancy will find that Brad feels he has to get a doctorate before he marries, thus he can't imagine getting married for at least another four years. Whatever she discovers, the information she acquires will help her plan her course and act wisely.

If Brad tells her he's not interested in marriage, she has solid grounds for making a decision: "Then I'm going to have to cut the amount of time I spend with you because I've got to get to know more guys." Or, "You're such a good friend. Even though it means I may never get married, I'm going to continue spending the same amount of time with you I've been spending all along."

Whatever Nancy decides, her decision will be based on solid information rather than vague hopes, dreams, and wishes.

"Nancy," I said, "you say you want to get married and you're frustrated in your relationship with Brad because nothing seems to be happening. Yet you also say you've never told him what your true desires are. I think you need to recognize that it is not Brad who is being unfair to you, but you who are being unfair to Brad. Your charges against him are unfounded.

"It is not his responsibility to tell you not to spend so much time with him. Nor is it his responsibility to bring up the subject of marriage. If he's not interested in marriage, he doesn't have to say anything to you about it. Even if he *is* interested in marriage, he is under no obligation to talk with you about it. He may be a *fool* not to say anything to you, but he's not treating you immorally or unethically by failing to bring up the subject.

"It's the same thing with you. You're under no moral obligation to tell Brad that you're interested in marriage. You may be a fool for not mentioning it. But you're not morally corrupt for failing to tell him about your interest. Just don't charge Brad with injustice when you are the one making a fool of yourself!"

In truth, if Brad were sensitive about these things and had a particularly bold character he would probably confront her on her behavior. He would probably notice that Nancy was spending an astonishingly large amount of time with him and so would ask her why. Or perhaps out of concern and caring he would tell her: "I think you're spending your time unwisely. I mean, I appreciate you doing all these things, but I can't imagine that it is the best use of your time to come over here as often as you do to cook my meals, wash my clothes, and do all the other things you do for me."

Of course, if Brad is at all aware of the cultural norms, he will probably recognize that Nancy's unsisterly ministrations (see chapter 2) are meant to imply an interest on her part in the idea of marriage. And so he might come right out and tell her, "Look, Nancy, I'm not interested in marriage right now." Or, "Boy, Nancy! I'd like us to get married, but that will have to wait for at least five years." Whatever he says, it will help Nancy make a wise choice for the future.

But again, ultimately, the point of my telling this story is that *Brad is under no obligation to Nancy*. Nancy is under obligation to the Lord for the way she spends her time. If she is wasting time with Brad, it is her responsibility, with or without Brad's aid, to stop the waste.

I made one more observation to Nancy concerning her behavior. "It strikes me, Nancy, that you've been deceitful. You've been trying to deceive Brad and maybe you've been trying to deceive yourself. While you've been pretending to be happy to be 'just friends' with Brad, 'just his sister,' in reality you've been becoming angry. Why? My guess is that you're not willing merely to be his sister. You want to be his wife. And so you've been attempting to trick Brad into feeling obligated to marry you.

"I don't want to put words in your mouth," I said, "but it seems to me you're almost to the point where you'd like to tell Brad, 'What? You won't marry me? After all I've done for you? After all the time I've spent?'"

"If it is possible," Ms. Elliot remarked, "it is, after a reasonable time . . . obligatory on the man to speak of getting married." If Ms. Elliot is correct, then the woman has a right to complain if the man fails to speak of getting married after "a reasonable time." "You've ripped me off!" the sister can complain. "I've spent all this time with you expecting us to get married, and now you're unwilling to make that kind of commitment."

But in fact, it is not the brother who is a thief because he refuses to make a commitment to his sister; it is the sister who is unjust in charging her brother with wrongdoing. If she is entering the relationship or proceeding in it with the idea of possibly getting married, then she should make her expectations and desires known.

"Maybe Brad is supposed to be your husband; maybe he isn't," I told Nancy. "Whatever is supposed to be, don't pretend to be satisfied as Brad's sister when what you really want is to be his wife. And above all, don't try to trick Brad into feeling *obligated* to be your husband! Deal with him forthrightly, with integrity and honesty. Tell him what you're thinking and ask him what he has in mind."

Brothers and sisters avoid trying to place others in positions of obligation. They speak forthrightly about their desires, expectations, and intentions, and they make sure they distinguish between interests, commitments, and obligations. If they are entering a relationship or proceeding in it with the thought or intent of getting married, they let the other person know, forthrightly, verbally: "I'm spending the time I am with you because I'm interested in marriage." They don't rely on inference and implication.

Questions for Study and Discussion

1. In Galatians 5:1 and 4:8–9, Paul tells us that "it is for freedom that Christ has set us free. Stand firm, then, and do not let yourselves be burdened again by a yoke of slavery. . . . Formerly, when you did not know God, you were slaves to those who by nature are not gods. But now that you know God—or rather are known by God—how is it that you are turning back to those weak and miserable principles?"

   Rewrite this passage to speak to the situation of brother-sister relationships before marriage. Why should you seek to avoid being owned by one of your brothers or sisters?

2. Using God's example, what kinds of responsibilities does ownership bring? (Read the passages as a basis for your answers.)

   a. For the owner? Isaiah 43:1–7; Hosea 11:1–4; Romans 5:8, 10.

   b. For the one owned? Exodus 20:2ff; Deuteronomy 5:6ff; 1 Corinthians 6:19–20; 2 Corinthians 5:14–15.

3. How do the responsibilities present in God's ownership of us carry over into the three other ownership relationships the Bible talks about?

   a. Parents and children. Deuteronomy 5:16; Ephesians 6:1–3; Colossians 3:20; and Deuteronomy 6:6–7; Ephesians 6:4; Colossians 3:21.

   b. Masters and slaves. Ephesians 6:5–8; Colossians 3:22–24; 1 Peter 2:18; and Ephesians 6:9; Colossians 4:1; James 5:1–6.

   c. Husbands and wives. 1 Corinthians 7:3, 33–34; Ephesians 5:21–33; 1 Peter 3:1–7.

4. Sometimes you'll hear a person say, "It's *my* body. I can do with it as I want." According to 1 Corinthians 6:19–20 and 7:4; Colossians 1:13; John 5:19; and Psalm 127:3, are these people speaking truthfully? Who owns you? Do ownership rights ever change over the course of your life?

5. This chapter suggests that because they can't adequately compensate each other for the costs of such a privilege, brothers and sisters should refrain from limiting each other's social contacts.

   a. How do you feel about that idea? Is it correct? Why or why not?

   b. If *brothers and sisters* can't adequately compensate each other for the privilege of limiting each other's social contacts, are *husbands and wives* able to pay the price? Why or why not?

   c. How about in the matter of sexual relations? God sets strict limits on who husbands and wives are supposed to have sex with (see 1 Corinthians 6:18; 7:2–5; Hebrews 13:4). What kind of compensation is there for husbands and wives to own each other in this realm?

d. Give some other examples besides sexual and social relations in which husbands and wives often exert ownership authority over each another.

e. Can the mutual ownership of a marriage relationship be a blessing? If so, how and to whom? If not, why not?

f. When can ownership become a curse rather than a blessing? (Answer this question for both the owned and the owner.)

6. Some men and women make demands like, "Unless you're willing to commit yourself to me, we're going to have to quit seeing each other. I just can't afford the time anymore. If we're going to keep spending time together, I need your commitment." Someone has pointed out that this demand sounds similar to the demand young men sometimes make: "Unless you're willing to have sex with me, we're going to have to quit dating. If you loved me, you'd be willing to go to bed with me."

a. How are these demands parallel? How are they different?

b. How is the one demanding the commitment likely to respond if the other refuses to comply? Why is he or she likely to respond this way?

c. Why is there no reason a young woman should feel compelled to have sex with her boyfriend?

d. Why is there no reason one brother or sister should ever feel compelled to make a commitment to another?

7. For what reasons is it legitimate for a man and woman to spend time together (any amount of time, from ten seconds a month to thirty hours a week)?

8. This chapter suggests that brothers and sisters avoid making commitments to one another to "pursue the possibility

of marriage." Yet, if they are entering into a relationship for that purpose, then they ought to make that plain.

a. Is it possible to *avoid making a commitment* to pursue the possibility of marriage and yet enter into a relationship *for that purpose?* If so, how?

b. Is it possible to *tell* someone that you're entering a relationship with the purpose of pursuing the possibility of marriage yet not make a *commitment* to them to pursue that possibility? If so, how is that possible?

c. By speaking about these matters, what distinctions are being made? Are they valid and useful distinctions? Why or why not?

9. When is it wise to turn down a gift—a date, time spent together, some form of service, whatever?

10. If one person tells another, "I'm spending time with you because I'm interested in marriage," is the person who receives this message obligated to express his or her own interest (or lack thereof) in the idea of marriage? Why or why not?

11. To what extent should a man and woman speak about their respective interests in marriage? In your opinion, what principles should limit their communication in this area?

12. If both men and women are owned by God and by their parents, what does this say about the tradition of a woman's father "giving her away" to the groom at the wedding? Should the groom, too, be given to his bride? Also, what does this say about premarital sexual intercourse? Who is sinned against when a couple gets sexually involved prior to marriage?

13. Having read this chapter, look again at your answers to question 1 (a) and (c) in the Introduction. Is your answer complete? Do you know any boyfriends or girlfriends or

participants in "serious" relationships who do *not* have a sense of ownership of or obligation to one another?

a. If so, how have they escaped such a feeling?

b. If not, do you believe such feelings of ownership or obligation are legitimate? Why do you or do you not believe they are legitimate?

14. In your opinion, when people feel as if they are being owned or are under obligation to another, where do those feelings come from?

No one is to approach any close relative to have sexual relations. I am the LORD. . . . Do not have sexual relations with your sister.

Leviticus 18:6, 9

You have heard that it was said, "Do not commit adultery." But I tell you that anyone who looks at a woman lustfully has already committed adultery with her in his heart.

Matthew 5:27–28

7

SEX

Brothers and Sisters Avoid Sexual Intimacy

John and Alice had a special relationship. It had taken a while, but over the past few months their physical relationship had grown to the point where every night they got together they would spend at least a few minutes (five, ten, fifteen minutes, or more) hugging and kissing. They were both satisfied with this state of affairs until one evening John became sexually stimulated enough by their activities that he felt compelled to ask Alice's forgiveness.

It was not as if he had "lost control" and tried to take advantage of Alice. If someone had taken a movie of their activities, John was convinced the cinematographer would have thought them tame. John never did anything more than hug or kiss Alice. His hands never wandered lower than her shoulders.

On the outside things were wonderful. Inside, however, John knew he was wrong. "We should have never done what we did last night," he told Alice. "I was wrong. I never want to get involved in that kind of physical intimacy in the future. Will you forgive me?"

"I don't understand," said Alice. "Why do I need to forgive you? We were just expressing our love."

"Maybe you were expressing love," John responded, "but for me it was lust." He reminded Alice of what Jesus had said about "anyone who looks at a woman lustfully has already committed adultery with her in his heart" (Matthew 5:28). "When I was with you last night, I wasn't loving you," he admitted. "I was lusting after you. I was pursuing all the sexual stimulation I thought I could get—and I was wrong."

Three Kinds of Physical Intimacy

Over the years I've discovered there are at least three types of physical intimacy. They don't necessarily take different physical forms; nonparticipants may not be able to distinguish successfully between them. But I've never met an adult who is wholly naive about the distinctions I'm about to make.

And so, though I will not try to provide a clinical description, I believe the various forms of intimacy I'm about to describe can be and ought to be distinguished. You need to make that distinction in order to avoid physical-sexual intimacy while engaging in physical-emotional and physical-social intimacy.

Brothers and sisters enjoy these latter two forms of physical intimacy; they refuse to participate in physical-sexual intimacy.

Physical-Social Intimacy

Physical-social intimacy is physical contact between two people that is demanded by social convention.

In my family when relatives come over and we greet one another, I'm expected to kiss the women. To be honest, I wish I didn't have to kiss some of them—for instance, my aunt whom I see maybe once every five years. I kiss her because the social context demands it. I have no sexual interest in her; I feel no emotional closeness to her; if anything, I feel an emotional barrier between us. She was the one who always made a scene when I was younger about my "atrocious manners." But I kiss her anyway because that's what's expected.

Some people kiss a person good-night on their first date because they think that's what the social context demands. It isn't that they have an overwhelming desire to kiss the other person; they aren't overcome by some great need to communicate an emotional message; they may not even particularly like the person. It's just that they believe "you're supposed to kiss your date when you say good-night." That's physical-social intimacy.

Physical-social intimacy is usually a highly stylized activity intended to convey a message of goodwill. We use these conventional behaviors in mundane, day-to-day kinds of situations: when two businessmen who don't know each other first meet, for example. In the United States they shake hands; in Japan they bow.

The term *physical-social intimacy* may cover some of the hugging that goes on in some church services and possibly even the kind of physical contact athletes engage in when they accidentally bump into one another in the midst of a game. The participants aren't thinking sex; there's little emotion involved. It's physical intimacy "demanded by the job" that says, "I'm pleased to be in your presence," or, minimally, "I'm willing to maintain peace in your presence." Brothers and sisters certainly want to convey these kinds of messages, so, whenever possible, they do their best to fulfill social conventions.

Physical-Emotional Intimacy

When people move out of the realm of strict social convention, they enter into either physical-emotional or physical-sexual intimacy. Note, for example, what happens when people ignore the social conventions and refuse to engage in such behavior: the negative power of the message conveyed in such a case would be strong enough to precipitate a relational crisis. In Western cultures, for instance, you don't refuse to shake the hand of a man to whom you're first being introduced. To refuse such a gesture is almost tantamount to saying, "I don't honor you. I'm willing to fight you." The recipient of the antisocial message will perceive a sullenness or condescension on the part of the one who refuses to shake his hand.

I would guess that probably 90 percent of the touch that goes on between football, baseball, basketball, and other athletes is physical-social intimacy. When these players touch, they're not trying to say anything of great import; they're just trying to play the game the best they can. They're "doing their job."

On the other hand, a second baseman may feel that his opponent just slid into second base with special vigor or with the intent to hurt him or to knock him off balance. *He's trying to intimidate me*, the second baseman may think. And, indeed, the runner's slide may have been meant to convey just such a message: *You'd better watch out, I'm a hard-charger!* There's a message with a strong negative emotional element. I call this physical-emotional intimacy.

At my mother's funeral my dad and I held hands as a way of comforting each other. We were saying something like, "I care. I'm here. I grieve with you. It's okay." Our physical intimacy didn't merely convey a message of mutual respect and goodwill. Rather, it served as an emotional outlet. It communicated a powerful emotional message that I doubt could have been expressed so well by any other means. Again: physical-emotional intimacy.

I get involved in physical-emotional intimacy when I kiss my children good-night or hold them when they're crying. Football players enjoy physical-emotional intimacy when, after a great play, they hug each other, jump up and down, and slap each other on the back. This kind of intimacy doesn't excite anyone; it isn't engaged in because the participants are of one gender or the other. The content of the emotional message is all that matters. Physical-emotional intimacy enables people to express their emotions to each other.

In many church circles I see a growing emphasis on the need for touch. According to John Trent and Gary Smalley, a recent study at UCLA found that "just to maintain emotional and physical health, men and women need eight to ten meaningful touches each day!"[1]

Physical contact for emotional needs is powerful. Michael E. Phillips, in an article titled "Appropriate Affection," describes several types of touch that I would place in the category of physical-emotional intimacy.[2] He tells the story of putting his arm around Ted, a man who weighed 360 pounds. "I [had] tried to show affection to Ted," Phillips says, "but he wasn't easy to get close to. . . . He kept pushing me away."

One day Ted called Phillips with an urgent need. "His pipes were leaking, . . . he knew nothing about plumbing, [and] he couldn't afford a plumber." Phillips solved the problem and at the end of the ordeal, "put my arm almost around Ted's shoulders and said I was glad to be of some assistance. At that, Ted began to cry like a baby. He said, 'No one has ever cared enough to put an arm around me.'"

In the church where I am now a member, I have found that, while blessing or praying for another person, if one touches him on the shoulder, head, back, leg, foot, hand—wherever one can touch a person without sexual overtones—the touch conveys a powerful, emotionally satisfying message.

Physical-emotional intimacy is like that; it can convey powerful messages of love and care, of being there for another person. Brothers and sisters use physical-emotional intimacy to encourage and build up, never to intimidate or communicate negative feelings.

Physical-Sexual Intimacy

When I held my father's hand during my mother's funeral, I was engaging in a kind of physical intimacy I could as easily engage in with my sister, my daughter, or anyone else to whom I am not married. There is a kind of hand-holding, however, I would never engage in with my father.

I do not remember, but I may have squeezed my father's hand while we sat there. I may have even intertwined my fingers in his. But the kind of squeezes, the frequency, the intensity, and the other hand motions we engaged in were far different from what my girlfriends and I once pursued or what I sometimes do now with Sarita.

With my girlfriends, I was a hand-holding artist. I was rarely satisfied merely to grip their hands the way I might shake the hand of a stranger or the way I would hold hands with a person I don't know but with whom I have been asked to join hands for prayer.

My girlfriends and I would intertwine our fingers. We would give each other "knowing" squeezes. We would caress and massage each other with our thumbs. There was a frequency of motion, an intensity, a sense of timing, that is totally different from normal, acceptable hand-holding behavior among other unmarried people . . . or brothers and sisters.

I call the kind of behavior my girlfriends and I engaged in physical-sexual intimacy. Physical-sexual intimacy is physical contact that communicates commitment. Not only does it say, "I'm here, I care, I love you (with a familial, brotherly love)," but, "I *will* here, I *will* care, I *will* love you (with the love of a husband)."

Beyond these messages, however, there is something else. When two people are involved in physical-sexual intimacy, they not only communicate propositional truth ("I will be here, I will care, I will love you"), but they move into another dimension of relationship altogether. Physical-sexual intimacy differs from physical-social and physical-emotional intimacy as time differs from space.

Burdette (Bud) Palmberg, for twenty years the pastor of Mercer Island Covenant Church near Seattle, Washington, put it this way:

> Our sexuality is the expression of God's intention for an entire relationship—intellectual intimacy, emotional intimacy, recreational intimacy, social intimacy, all of these things. Sex is a physical expression of a much larger reality. . . . It's a natural and God-given part of a whole relationship, . . . the final part of a completely intimate relationship.[3]

Physical-sexual intimacy, instead of being just one more building block within the structure of a relationship, actually expresses that relationship's completion. It is the capstone of a relationship, the fulfillment of intimacy. When a man and woman engage in physical-sexual intimacy, they are expressing wholeness, oneness. The Apostle Paul, for example, says that through sexual intercourse, even illicit sexual intercourse, a man and woman communicate their sense of union with one another. "Do you not know that he who unites himself with a prostitute is one with her in body?" he asks (1 Corinthians 6:16).

It seems highly ironic to me that in common parlance today, the term *sexual intercourse* is used merely to refer to the physical act of a man's penis penetrating a woman's vagina and then ejaculating. Many authors, even Christian ones, thus speak of a couple being "sexually active" only *after* they have come together in this fashion. As if sexual intercourse occurs only when penetration occurs!

The word *intercourse*, unmodified, simply means commerce, communication, or dealing between two parties. Two people can deal with one another in a sexual manner long before their genitals come into contact, just as two parties must be involved in economic intercourse long before they ever sign a contract, or they may be engaged in social intercourse before ever meeting face-to-face. Behavior can be sexual in nature even when two people never come into physical contact. What else is one to call the flirtatious smile, the sexy voice, or the facial expression many people refer to as "bedroom eyes"?

Physical-sexual intimacy is not the same as sexual intercourse in the narrow sense of penetration and ejaculation, nor is it the same as sexual intercourse in the broad sense of "every type of sexual dealing between two people." Rather, physical-sexual intimacy is *sexual behavior that involves physical contact*. That's why it's *physical*-sexual intimacy and not merely *sexual* intimacy. Physical-sexual intimacy can include anything from the caress of a finger upon a sleeve, to hand-holding, to coitus.

If I may be granted the indulgence of expressing a truism: Physical-sexual intimacy is *physical contact designed to stimulate a sexual response*—to move a relationship, if it is not already there, into the sexual sphere. Though it is designed to stimulate a sexual response, for various reasons—including previous experience, social custom, and physical makeup—one or the other of the participants may be insensitive or desensitized to the stimulation physical-sexual intimacy provides. Dwight Hervey Small points out that "holding hands is a form of stimulation that has [a] tolerance point . . . where diminishing returns make an urgent demand for something more. Kissing and embracing follow and in turn have their own tolerance point. Then the demand is for caressing . . . leading on eventually to petting, to manipulation of the erogenous zones to excite full sexual arousal."[4]

The idea is, after you've held hands for awhile, you want something more. So you move into kissing and embracing. But once you're into kissing and embracing, hand-holding no longer holds the stimulative power it once did. Certainly once you're involved in petting and "manipulation of the erogenous zones," hand-holding has little stimulative power!

Ken Wilson, pastor of Emmaus Fellowship in Ann Arbor, Michigan, however, says he finds it easy "to demonstrate to a young man that the sexual 'preliminaries' are in fact part of the total package of the sexual encounter [and, therefore, part of physical-sexual intimacy]. . . . I simply ask him if he has ever had an erection while necking with his girlfriend."[5]

Finally, if I may attempt to express it in one more, slightly different way: physical-sexual intimacy is *physical contact with another person engaged in or enjoyed specifically because the person with whom one is making contact is a sexual being*; the person's gender makes a difference.

André Bustanoby, a marriage and family therapist, points this out when he tells pastoral counselors, "We have to be totally honest with ourselves. Motive is the key. Do we touch [physically or verbally] out of sexual attraction, out of an inner desire to exploit the situation, or do we touch out of a spontaneous expression of care for that person, quite apart from gender?"[6]

Brothers and sisters and pastoral counselors can legitimately touch from the latter motives; not from the former. Bustanoby concludes: "When you touch with sex on your mind, you set the stage for sexual exploitation, whether you touch with words or with body contact."[7] I would merely want to clarify: you not only "set the stage" for sexual exploitation, you are *involved* in sexually exploitative behavior.

Brothers and sisters in the Lord recognize that the same rules that govern interactions between unmarried family members and members of their own sex must govern their interactions with members of the opposite sex outside their families as well. Brothers and sisters in the Lord avoid physical-sexual intimacy and, indeed, sexual intimacy of all types.

But . . . !

In *Dating, Sex and Friendship*, Joyce Huggett calls oral sex, mutual masturbation, and heavy petting "question mark areas" for a relationship between an unmarried man and woman. "On biblical authority," she says, "I have the right to say to you that genital intercourse outside of marriage is wrong. I have no *biblical* authority for dictating to you where you draw the petting line" (emphasis hers).[8] In case you're wondering what she is referring to when she speaks of petting, she defines her terms: "By heavy petting I mean the practice of slipping your hands inside a girl's dress to fondle her breasts; or undoing the zip of your boyfriend's trousers to fondle his genitals; or stroking your girlfriend's thighs or genitalia. Heavy petting includes lying together in a state of undress. . . ."[9] Light petting, she says, is "fondling one another's breasts and genitals outside the clothes . . . also . . . any form of lying together."[10] Light petting, apparently, isn't a "question mark area."

If Huggett is right, the Bible is silent about the practices she has so graphically described for us. *Genital intercourse*, she says, is forbidden to unmarried couples. But sexual intercourse in the broad sense of the term or physical-sexual intimacy of other kinds? No way!

Other authors, too, are uncomfortable when it comes to defining what's right and wrong in the sexual arena. The most recent example I happened to run across came from Josh McDowell. In *Love, Dad*, McDowell says he draws "The Line" defining right and wrong, good and bad, acceptable and unacceptable behavior between "Casual Kissing (Peck Kissing)" and "Prolonged Kissing." "For whatever my personal opinion is worth," he says, "there it is. I don't believe most healthy Christians in a dating relationship . . . can progress much beyond this line without asking for trouble. . . . Past this point you begin to arouse in each other desires that cannot be righteously fulfilled outside of marriage."[11]

Put another way, the best McDowell can offer is his personal opinion, and his personal opinion is based on fear: what is *likely* to happen among *most* healthy Christians in a dating relationship.

If you were to read enough authors like Huggett and McDowell, you would think they were right: we really are left to our own opinions when it comes to determining what is right and wrong. But Huggett and McDowell are not correct; God *has* given us guidelines, and brothers and sisters pay attention to them.

In 1 Corinthians 6:18 Paul says, "Flee from sexual immorality. All other sins a man commits are outside his body, but he who sins sexually sins against his own body."

The Greek word *porneia* is what is translated *sexual immorality* in the New International Version. Lest there be any question about what Paul meant when he said, "Flee from *porneia*," *The Interpreter's Dictionary of the Bible,* says it refers to "every kind of sexual intercourse outside of marriage."[12] Ken Wilson is more explicit: "The prohibition of *porneia* completely rules out a wide range of sexual interaction [such as]. . . necking, making out, petting . . . [and] much of what would be considered foreplay."[13]

But even ignoring this explicit and wide-ranging prohibition, God has called His people to treat each other as brothers and sisters. Those who have committed themselves to obey God in this matter will take note of what the Bible says concerning the way brothers and sisters are supposed to treat each other.

Leviticus 18:6 and 9 says, "No one is to approach any close relative to have sexual relations. . . . Do not have sexual relations with your sister."

Little research is required to discover that God is referring to far more here in Leviticus 18 than merely the act that Huggett refers to as genital intercourse. If we were to look at the Hebrew, we would find that the New International Version translators paraphrased rather drastically. Leviticus 18:6 and 9 say something quite a bit more forceful than merely "avoid sexual relations." A more literal translation would have verse 6 say, "No one is to approach any close relative to uncover [his] nakedness." And verse 9: "Do not uncover the nakedness of your sister."

Can Huggett seriously suggest that when a couple is involved in oral sex, mutual masturbation, and heavy petting, they are *not* involved in uncovering one another's nakedness? Even by her definition of light petting: does the fact that a couple keeps their clothes on make any difference? Suppose they were to take off their clothes when they engaged in their petting activities, but did so only when they were in a darkened room. Would that be acceptable? (Their sense of visual input concerning each other's nakedness would be the same as if they left their clothes on!) How about if they were to disrobe but place gloves on their hands? The tactile stimulation would be the same as if they kept their clothes on.

There is a problem with Huggett's line of reasoning . . . and with the reasoning of virtually every author who tries to draw lines within the spectrum of sexual behavior. *Their focus is wrong.* Whether an act is righteous or not depends not, as McDowell would have us understand, on the willpower of the participants or how dangerous the activity becomes. It has nothing to do with whether a man's penis comes within ten miles, four millimeters, or two microns of a woman's vagina. The righteousness of an act has little to do with the act's outward form—whether clothes are off or on and whether or not a couple wears gloves. Instead, as Bustanoby suggested, it has to do with the act's *meaning* and the heart attitudes of those who engage in it.

Not What You Do So Much as What You Mean

As I look at Scripture I find God places less emphasis on the outward form of our activities than on the *significance* those activities hold for the persons engaging in them. For instance, if one studies the passages of Scripture where the sins of adultery and fornication are addressed (see, for example, Malachi 2:13–16; 1 Corinthians 6:15–20; 7:3–4; and Hebrews 13:4), one finds that God never condemns these practices for the kinds of reasons so often put forward in our society—because a baby might be born out of wedlock or because there is a danger of contracting venereal disease or AIDS. Important as these potential physical outcomes may be, God always seems to emphasize the *meaning* of the sexual intimacy, what the sexual intimacy *communicates*. The morality of an act is in its meaning more than an acts form or physical result.

I am not suggesting that if God has forbidden an act—say, eating the fruit of the tree of the knowledge of good and evil—and we find ourselves unable to decipher the meaning of that activity, we can therefore engage in it. Form and meaning are both important. All I am saying is that morality seems more tied to relationship and communication than to its form or physical consequences.

Small says virtually the same thing: "Any act is what it is because of its *meaning* to the persons involved."[14] On the basis of this insight, he happens to attack the practice of petting:

> Two persons engaged in petting can hardly say with honesty that there is less meaning than in actual intercourse, for mentally they have touched with the most intimate meaning. By touch and imagination they have invaded the inmost precincts of each other's personal and sexual being. The bodily secret of both has been revealed. Actual intercourse would add little beside the possibility of pregnancy. So one must conclude that the Christian view of petting is to put it on the same moral level as intercourse itself.[15]

By limiting his comments to the matter of petting, however, and by focusing too quickly on what actual intercourse would add to the experience of petting, Small fails to point out that if "any act is what it is because of its meaning to the persons involved," not only is petting on the same moral level as actual intercourse, but *every act* is on the same moral level as coitus *if it is engaged in with the same purpose and for the same ends as one engages in coitus.*

And what are the ends and purposes of coitus? In 1 Corinthians 6, Paul says, "Do you not know that he who unites himself with a prostitute is one with her in body? . . . You are not your own; you were bought at a price. Therefore honor God with your body" (1 Corinthians 6:16, 19–20). If Paul is correct, then no matter what other meanings the participants may want to attach to it, God views coitus as a vehicle by which a man and woman declare their loyalty to and unity and oneness with each other.

Within the context of marriage, God says, such a declaration is valid; it is appropriate, honorable, right, pure, lovely, of good repute (Philippians 4:8).

If you are not married, however; if you cannot marry or have no intention of marrying the person with whom you're engaging in sexual intercourse, then your declaration is inappropriate, dishonorable, immoral, impure, something to be avoided at all costs. You're communicating false messages every time you engage in it.

Beyond the dishonest nature of the messages the participants communicate to one another, there is another problem with sexual intercourse outside of marriage. When a man and woman unite themselves outside of marriage, Paul says, they are declaring their independence from God. "You are not your own; you were bought at a price. Therefore honor God with your body," he writes. But the person who refuses to obey His master is saying, "No! I refuse to acknowledge God's right to own me." Not only so, but, "I am willing to be dependent on (owned by and obligated to) the woman (or man) with whom I am engaging in sexual immorality!"

Consider why Joseph responded as he did to Potiphar's wife when she urged him to go to bed with her. He didn't say, "How could I do such a wicked thing and sin against *your husband?*"

Rather, he said, "How . . . could I do such a wicked thing and sin against *God?*" (Genesis 39:9, emphasis mine). If Joseph had assented to the demands of Potiphar's wife, he would have been indicating his independence from God and his dependence on her. He was unwilling to do that.

Joseph's fear, apparently, was not so much that he might raise Potiphar's wrath but that he would be sinning against God. And, indeed, we know he would have been sinning in at least three ways: He would have been pledging his allegiance to Potiphar's wife ("I am one with you"). He would have been lying to her, implying by his declaration of allegiance that he had a *right* to unite himself to her (which, of course, he did not). Further, or perhaps even *prior* to this implied lie concerning his right to make a pledge, the pledge itself ("I am one with you") would have been false since Joseph knew he was *not* one with Potiphar's wife and had no intention of becoming one with her. Finally, if Joseph had acceded to this woman's demands, he would have been declaring rebellion against God ("I do not care what God says, I will do whatever I want").

Joseph wanted to do none of these things and so he refused to engage in physical-sexual intimacy with Potiphar's wife.

As I said in chapter 4, brothers and sisters have no business communicating by their actions what they would never say with words. They have no business lying to or deceiving or misleading one another.

Also, brothers and sisters avoid obligating themselves to one another or trying to obligate one another to themselves (see chapter 6).

And as we discussed in chapter 2, brothers and sisters treat each other the same when single as they do when married. If it is illegitimate for them to communicate a certain level of commitment to one another after they are married to other persons, then it is illegitimate to communicate that level of commitment to one another before they are married or before they have any intention of marrying each other. If it would be illegitimate for them to be involved sexually with one another after they are married to other persons, then it is also illegitimate for them to be involved sexually *before* they are married.

Finally, brothers and sisters remember their purpose, to bless others (see chapter 1) and they obey God because they trust Him to meet all their needs and to fulfill their hearts' desires (see chapter 9).

Brothers and sisters focus not on, "How far can I go before I'm out-of-bounds?" Rather, "How close can I come to the goal God has set for me?" Not, "How much can I get for myself?" but, "How much blessing can I give?" For brothers and sisters, the blessing they try to give is long-term and permanent, not the "blessing" of momentary bodily thrills.

God tells us His will—"that you should be holy; that you should avoid sexual immorality; that each of you should learn to control his own body in a way that is holy and honorable, not in passionate lust like the heathen, who do not know God; and that in this matter no one should wrong his brother or take advantage of him" (1 Thessalonians 4:3–6).

"Put to death . . . whatever belongs to your earthly nature: sexual immorality [*porneia*], impurity, lust, evil desires," we're warned in Colossians 3:5. Paul tells Timothy to "flee the evil desires of youth, and pursue righteousness, faith, love and peace" (2 Timothy 2:22).

Are you pursuing these goals? Skilled drivers know that when driving on a mountain road, the best place to focus is not on the guardrails at the edge of the cliff; the best place to focus is on the center line. If you're worried about falling over the edge of the cliff when it comes to your relationships with members of the opposite sex, quit looking at the guardrail—"how far you can go"; keep your eye on the center line: God's purpose for your life and relationships.

Treating Each Other as Brother and Sister

Brothers and sisters may be physically intimate—physically-*emotionally* or physically-*socially* intimate—but they avoid physical-sexual intimacy. They avoid sexual intimacy of all types. If they become sexually intimate, they know they have crossed the bounds of appropriate behavior for a relationship between a brother and sister, and they know they need to ask each other's forgiveness. Sexual intimacy is not a normal, acceptable, or healthy form of interaction between brothers and sisters.

For Sarita and me, treating each other as brother and sister meant we never held hands and didn't kiss until after we were engaged. There were no social contexts or emotional situations that required such behavior. Hugs were generally taboo as well.

Notice my choice of words. I said there was no situation that *required* such behavior. While I was in college, my sexual urges were so strong that I deliberately refused to touch women except in situations where a touch seemed absolutely necessary. Especially with women like Sarita—women toward whom I was romantically attracted or who were romantically attracted to me—I figured the danger of becoming physically-sexually intimate was too great to allow me to enter easily into any physical contact. When a person's romantic desires are involved, the dividing wall between social, emotional, and sexual intimacy is too easy to miss. The distinction could hinge on nothing more than the split second it took Carrie and me to realize that our hand-holding as we ran down the hill had continued a moment longer than regular friends would have allowed (see Introduction).

The upshot: as far as I was concerned, when I was with a girl toward whom I was especially attracted, it was not enough that a situation *allowed* physical-emotional or physical-social intimacy or that it made these forms of intimacy seem like a good idea. I was convinced that the situation had to *demand* such intimacy before I would pursue it.

There were other women with whom I engaged in physical-emotional intimacy a little more readily: a girl who had just found out that her parents were going to get a divorce, for instance. I gently held her hand as she sobbed quietly and recounted the details. And then there were the girls whom I felt free to hug or touch in greeting—generally a sideways hug (shoulder-to-shoulder) or a touch or squeeze of the upper arm. At most, a quick, one-two-three kneading of the shoulder muscle.

Since many women seem to be ignorant of how men's minds work (and few men are willing to talk about it), I might as well say that, as a red-blooded male, I was often far too aware of how a woman's body would press against mine—even for those who were relatively flat-chested—to be able to say honestly that a frontal hug would be a harmless, chaste activity!

In Matthew 5:27–28, Jesus says, "You have heard that it was said, 'Do not commit adultery.' But I tell you that anyone who looks at a woman lustfully has already committed adultery with her in his heart." It is not only the legitimacy of our *acts* that we must consider, but the purity of our *hearts*. My heart generally needed no more stimulation than that which shoulder-to-shoulder and arm-to-shoulder kinds of contact with my sisters might provide!

I don't mean to make this into a rule. I didn't always avoid frontal hugs. I didn't always need to. Nor am I saying that the particular behavioral standards I set for myself are universally valid. All men are not the same as I am. All situations are not the same. There are ways to hug from the front without acquiring breast-to-breast contact.

I am, however, trying to illustrate the extent to which our behavior may need to be limited if we are to remain right and pure before God. As Jesus put it, "If your right hand causes you to sin, cut it off" (Matthew 5:30). If frontal hugs can cause you to sin, you need to avoid them. Is there some other behavior that will likely cause you trouble? Avoid it as well!

Interestingly, I discovered on more than one occasion that even if I was totally pure in my motives for engaging in physical-emotional intimacy with a woman and even if we had shown no romantic interest in one another before this contact, if the intimacy was deep enough or the emotional messages strong enough, I subsequently had to make explicit denials that I had any further romantic, sexual intentions toward her. As Burdette Palmberg put it, "When we begin to develop intimacy with someone, there's going to be a natural tendency toward a sexual expression. . . . Any time you become emotionally involved with a person, you're moving into the arena of sexual temptation. You're touching one of the springs from which our sexuality comes to the surface."[16]

Brothers and sisters proceed with great caution when it comes to physical-emotional intimacy and seek to avoid physical-sexual intimacy altogether.

"And If I Blow It?"

Despite what I've said, the fact is, I did not always avoid sexual intimacy with my sisters in the Lord. Several times I did things a brother should never do.

There was the night Sarita and I went for a walk and wound up out on a high school baseball field. We sat down in the dugout. I should say, Sarita sat down. I laid down on the bench next to her and put my head in her lap.

Foolish man that I was! That's not the kind of thing a brother does; it's not the kind of thing one man does to another. No *friends* I know ever put their heads in each other's laps. It's not something a married man should do to a woman other than his wife. That's lovers' behavior, the kind of thing that says, "You're mine. I'm yours. We're one." As Sarita's brother I had no business treating her that way. In laying my head in her lap I failed to live up to my obligation to treat her as my sister. And so I had to admit I was wrong and ask for her forgiveness.

Then there was the day I went for a walk with Cathy. I showed my "friendship" by putting my arm around her. It wasn't a brief, friendly squeeze: "Hi! It's good to be here with you." It was the lingering intimacy of a lover. For fifteen minutes or more, maybe half an hour, we walked side by side, arms around each other. Every now and then I would squeeze her close to my side.

I had no business treating her like that. I had no business treating her like that before I was married to Sarita. I had no business treating her like that after I was married to Sarita. I was communicating all the wrong things, the false commitments of a lover. I was not treating her as my sister. And again I was wrong. And again I had to admit my failure, seek forgiveness, and move on.

I tell you these stories neither to prove my righteousness nor to show what a great sinner I am. I am human. I was not and am not perfect. I have succumbed to temptation. I have sinned. More importantly than that, however, when I sinned, I asked God's forgiveness, and asked my sisters to forgive me as well. Having been forgiven, I moved on. When you sin, when any of us sins: when we fail to live up to our commitments, we have a God who forgives and who tells us to seek forgiveness. "If we confess our sins, he is faithful and just and will forgive us our sins and purify us from all unrighteousness" (1 John 1:9).

You say you've already sinned, and not only that, but have sinned far worse than I? It doesn't matter: God is still the same; He is still "the compassionate and gracious God, slow to anger, abounding in love and faithfulness, maintaining love to thousands, and forgiving wickedness, rebellion and sin" (Exodus 34:6–7; see also Joel 2:13; Jonah 4:2). When you sin, He is there to forgive.

But having been forgiven, move on. "Go and sin no more!" For while our God is slow to anger and quick to forgive, He is also the God who "does not leave the guilty unpunished" (Exodus 34:7) and who is displeased by those who shrink back from doing what is right (see Hebrews 10:38; Revelation 3:1–3, 15–16).

Questions for Study and Discussion

1. Many Christian authors seem to agree with Joyce Huggett about what constitutes questionable behavior in relationships between unmarried men and women (see above). They don't necessarily approve of these behaviors, they just don't see any scriptural grounds for declaring unequivocally: "These behaviors are wrong." Having read this chapter, what are your opinions?

a. Are oral sex, mutual masturbation, and heavy petting appropriate behaviors for brothers in the flesh to engage in with their sisters in the flesh? Why or why not?

b. Is "fondling one another's breasts and genitals outside the clothes" (*light petting* by Huggett's definition) appropriate behavior between brothers in the flesh and their sisters? Again: why or why not?

c. How about cuddling? Prolonged kissing? Full-mouth kissing?

d. Are these practices acceptable between brothers and sisters in the Lord?

e. Ultimately, what are the issues we must deal with here in this matter of sexual intimacy?

2. Concerning the three forms of physical intimacy described in this chapter (social, emotional, and sexual):

a. How are they the same?

b. How are they different?

c. *Why* are they different? What makes them different?

d. In practice, is it possible to confuse them? Can you think of any examples where people have confused them?

e. What could happen if someone mistook physical-sexual intimacy for physical-emotional or physical-social intimacy?

f. What if they mistook physical-emotional or physical-social intimacy for physical-sexual intimacy?

3. Many authors assume people are not sexually involved or active until they have passed the kissing, hugging, and hand-holding stage. What do you think? Explain your position.

    a. Is it possible to hold hands with another person in a sexual manner? Have you ever been stimulated sexually as a result of holding hands?

    b. When does physical intimacy become sexual in nature?

    c. When does it become immoral? (Make sure you explain what makes it immoral. Use Scripture if possible.)

4. Once people begin "going together" they will normally refuse to hold hands with other members of the opposite sex.

    a. Why do you think that is?

    b. Based on your answer to (a), are there any reasons you think God would want you to avoid hand-holding with members of the opposite sex outside of a marriage commitment? If so, what are they and under what circumstances do they apply?

5. People involved in boyfriend-girlfriend and "serious" dating relationships are usually very uncomfortable if their partners won't at least hold hands with them, let alone hug or kiss them.

    a. Do you know any boyfriends, girlfriends, or "serious" daters who do *not* engage in some form of physical-sexual intimacy? If you do, describe these people's relationships: why do they refuse to get involved sexually? If you don't know any such people, why do you think that is?

    b. What do a man and woman communicate to each other when they hold hands in public?

    c. What do they communicate to their friends?

    d. If they hold hands in the presence of their parents, what are they saying to their parents?

6. Do you disagree with this chapter's view of sexual intimacy? If you disagree, explain what it is you disagree with and why.

7. In Luke 17:1–2, Jesus said, "Things that cause people to sin are bound to come, but woe to that person through whom they come. It would be better for him to be thrown into the sea with a millstone tied around his neck than for him to cause one of these little ones to sin." Romans 14:13, 19 says, "Make up your mind not to put any stumbling block or obstacle in your brother's way. . . . therefore make every effort to do what leads to peace and to mutual edification." The principle of showing equal concern for all members of the body would teach us similar things.

    a. With these Scriptures and Scriptural principles as background, what principle(s) of conduct would you want to formulate for yourself in the area of sexual intimacy?

    b. If you and your brother or sister have a difference in response to sexual stimuli, what is your responsibility?

    c. Will God hold you responsible for your behavior if you happen not to be aware of your brother's or sister's response rate?

8. Some schools used to have "no touching" or "ten-inch separation" rules regarding guy-girl relationships. You were not to touch a member of the opposite sex or you were required to maintain at least a ten-inch distance between you and a member of the opposite sex.

    a. Why do you think the schools made such rules? What do you think they were trying to accomplish?

    b. If a man and woman were to obey these kinds of rules, what types of problems would they avoid? What problems could still arise?

    c. Do you think such rules would make good sense today? Why or why not?

9. When writing about relationships between men and women, most authors today spend a great deal of time talking about the limits a couple should place on their physical relationship: how much time they should spend together, what behaviors are acceptable, what are not. Rather than focusing on the specific *behavior*, we need to focus on the behavior's *meaning*.

   a. Do you think it's possible to determine a behavior's meaning? If not, why not? If so, how would you go about doing such a thing?

   b. What do you think of the idea that *meaning* more than *behavior* determines an activity's morality?

10. In Proverbs 5—9, Solomon seems to say that "to be wise" has a very simple definition. All you have to do is avoid one particular sin. What is that sin? Using Proverbs 5—9, and any other knowledge you may have, suggest reasons it is wise to avoid it.

11. Define and, to the extent that they are different, differentiate between:

   a. Friendly affection

   b. Romantic interest or attraction

   c. Sexual interest or attraction

   d. Sexual activity

   e. Sexual involvement

   f. Sexual intercourse

   g. Physical-sexual intimacy

   h. Coitus

   i. Physical-emotional intimacy

   j. Physical-social intimacy

12. Assume a person named Ron confessed that sometimes his sex drive becomes too much for him: "When I'm like that, all I think about is sex. But if I have sex with a girl, then I'm okay again for a couple of weeks, maybe—or less."

Use 1 Corinthians 7:2–5 to help you answer the following questions:

a. If Ron were married, what solution to his problem does God offer him?

b. For single people, is physical-sexual intimacy outside of marriage a satisfactory or Biblically acceptable alternative? Why or why not?

c. Is masturbation a satisfactory or Biblically acceptable alternative? Why or why not?

Let us not give up meeting together, as some are in the habit of doing, but let us encourage one another—and all the more as you see the Day approaching.

Hebrews 10:25

I have written you in my letter not to associate with sexually immoral people—not at all meaning the people of this world who are immoral, or greedy and swindlers, or idolaters. In that case you would have to leave this world. But now I am writing you that you must not associate with anyone who calls himself a brother but is sexually immoral or greedy, an idolater or a slanderer, a drunkard or a swindler. With such a man do not even eat.

1 Corinthians 5:9–11

8

DAY TIME, NIGHT TIME, LOTS OF TIME

Brothers and Sisters Spend Time Together

Mike and I were best friends in high school. We spent hours together. If Mike wanted to see me, he rarely called before coming over. He would just walk up to our front door, ring the bell, and ask, "Is John in?" It didn't matter what shape I was in, how fashionably I was dressed, or what I was doing. If I was home and didn't have responsibilities to attend to, we would get together.

Mike didn't come over to evaluate me. He never came to find out if I was as good-looking in private as I seemed to be in public. He didn't try to surprise me so he could discover what other friends I might have or what "competition" he might face for my affection. He came to my house because he wanted to be with me. And I went to his house for the same reason—because I wanted to be with him.

Mike and I did all kinds of things together. Sometimes our activities were focused, as when we planned and carried out an eighty-mile bike ride. Sometimes they weren't focused at all. We would sit around and talk—no preset purpose, no direction, just talk. Sometimes we would visit friends. Occasionally we would listen to music. We worked together and earned money by picking apples. We went ice skating on a nearby pond when it froze up in the middle of winter. Side by side, we tore our bicycles apart, overhauled them, and put them back together again. We talked about homework assignments and girls. We shared just about everything that popped into our minds.

Over time, Mike and I came to know each other's character, habits, likes, and dislikes. We came to know how we picked up our rooms, how we worked, how we studied, and how we related to our parents. We came to know each other intimately. . . as brothers. Perhaps even better than brothers. Mike and I were friends.

Relationships between brothers and sisters in Christ can be at least as good as Mike's and my relationship, and for the same reason: because *brothers and sisters spend time together*—lots of time, different kinds of time, time that they've made, time they've redeemed, and *always*, time that shows them for who they really are.

Brothers and Sisters Spend Time Together

Different Kinds of Time

Brothers and sisters don't limit themselves to Friday night movies or meals at fancy restaurants. They don't make special efforts to dress up for each other, "putting the best foot forward." They live life together the way they really are. Brothers and sisters go shopping together. They wash cars, eat meals, rake leaves, go for bike rides, work in the nursery—do virtually anything together except those things God has commanded them to avoid.

Taking my cues from my relationship with Mike, while I was in college I would sometimes drop in on my sisters unannounced—not to startle them, but because I figured that's the way friends act. And isn't that true? If a friend happens to be walking by, wouldn't he stop to say hello?

Most of the time this kind of behavior worked fine. But more than once I inadvertently showed up at one of my sister's doors just after she had gotten ready for bed (at 8:30 or 9:00 on a Thursday evening!), or when she was sick with the flu, or in the middle of a term paper. A couple of times I showed up when she was out with another guy.

But so what? It didn't matter. Not to me. I wasn't there to check up on her. I wasn't trying to "guard my territory" or to find out who she was going out with. I didn't visit guys for those purposes; I didn't visit my sisters for those purposes either. I visited my sisters because I wanted to bless them—to find out how they were doing and to show that I cared.

"Oh!" some women say. "*You* didn't mind. But how did your sisters feel? If you dropped in on me like that, I'd be mad!"

And I ask, Why? Brothers and sisters in the flesh haven't always showered and shaved before they bump into each other in the morning. They're not always in the best of health when they are in each other's presence. They don't always have their hair combed, their rooms picked up, and their lives in order. Sometimes their lives are downright messy. That doesn't mean they should stay away from each other. If anything, brothers and sisters need each other most when their lives are least "together."

I'm not suggesting brothers and sisters in Christ should ignore appearances or relish sloppiness. I'm merely saying that they don't—and, I believe, shouldn't—limit their contacts to only those times when they are "at their best," whatever their "best" may be. Indeed, if brothers and sisters are to minister effectively one to another, if they are to pray for and bless each other and offer words of encouragement, it is probably best that they *don't* see each other only when they are in high spirits, neatly groomed, and in perfect health. One can hardly pray realistically for other people if one never sees their needs.

Brothers and sisters spend different kinds of time together.

Make Time for One Another

If brothers and sisters are going to bless each other, they have to spend time together. And if they are going to spend time together, they often have to strategize how best to make that happen.

In most families, the demands of day-to-day life rarely allow us to make special arrangements for one another. There just isn't time. Therefore, we must use ordinary activities as a means to build relationships. In my family, if one of us is going shopping and the other wants to talk, we'll go shopping together. If one of us needs to do laundry and the other has to buy some socks, we'll go to the laundry and the department store together and talk along the way.

Sarita and I like to finish our Christmas shopping before Thanksgiving. If we can be done by August, so much the better. Our attitude toward Christmas shopping, however, means we always have some shopping to do that requires more than a quick jaunt down to the local supermarket.

So, rather than spending our time—not to mention money—on entertainment (hardly the best way to encourage conversations and mutual understanding!), Sarita and I often go shopping together on Friday nights. At 9:00 P.M. when the stores close, we go to a local pie shop and have some pie.

Friday evenings are times when we do some of our best talking. For very little more expense than a movie or concert, and with far fewer distractions, Sarita and I are able to enjoy each other's company, have a significant time for conversation, and accomplish a practical goal as well. Can you imagine a better deal than that?

Redeem the Time

One February afternoon after six weeks of gray skies, snow, and temperatures in the lower teens, the sun actually shone and the thermometer climbed up to twenty-nine degrees in East Lansing, Michigan. The floor under the back seat of my Mustang had rusted out. So had the trunk. Even the frame of the car had rusted through at one point. To this day I don't know what was holding that vehicle together. One thing I did know, however: unless I washed off the snow and the salt that was accumulating on the car's bottom, my beloved vehicle's demise would come sooner than I wanted.

I had a choice: I could go to the car wash alone, or I could invite a friend. If I went alone, I would get the car washed. If I went with a friend, I would get the car washed and also enjoy the companionship and conversation. I decided to invite a friend.

Which friend to invite? I decided to call Mary.

"Hi," I said. "You want to wash my car with me?"

"Sure!"

We went down to the local spray-and-wash and tried to get the salt off before it refroze to the car's underside and body.

"You asked a girl out to wash your car?" people exclaim.

"Absolutely. Is there anything wrong with it?"

"Well, it's . . . it's. . . ."

Go ahead. Say it. It's counter-cultural, . . . but absolutely Biblical . . . and *better* than the culture.

Asking a sister to come wash my car with me shows no disdain for her. If anything, it shows great concern: I want to spend time with you. So what if it's cold outside? So what if we get dirty? We get to spend almost an hour together we wouldn't spend otherwise.

Asking a sister in Christ to wash my car with me is the kind of thing biological brothers and sisters will do. It's the kind of thing a friend will do with his friend. It's the kind of thing that helps improve the time- and cost-effectiveness of building relationships. And it shows equal concern for other members of the body.

I could have washed my car just as easily with a male friend. I've washed my car with male friends. That day I happened to call Mary.

Brothers and sisters redeem the time.

Live Reality

Robbie and Kevin once came to me with a problem. They said they didn't know how to approach girls and ask them out for a

date. I asked them what they were going to be doing the coming
Friday night.

"Probably go down to an auto parts store to buy some parts,"
Kevin answered.

"Sounds good to me," I said. "Why not invite some girls to go
along?"

"What?!" They looked at me incredulously.

"Well?" I encouraged them.

"But . . .!"

"'But' what? Would you enjoy the girls' company?"

"Yes, but . . ."

"Do you think the girls would enjoy your company?"

"Maybe."

"Well?"

They looked at each other.

"Think of it this way," I suggested. "What if the girls invited
you to go along with them to buy groceries? Would you be offended?"

"No."

"Then why should they be offended if you invite them to go
with you to buy auto parts?"

"I don't know," they answered.

"Why not do both: they'll buy auto parts with you and you'll
buy food with them? How's that sound? Maybe after you're done
shopping, you can go out for a pizza together."

What I suggested Robbie and Kevin do is the kind of thing a
guy can do with another guy; it's the kind of thing two women
can do together. It's the kind of thing a husband and wife would
do if they wanted to spend more time with one another. And it's
the kind of thing brothers will do with their sisters.

Brothers and sisters live reality.

But What About the Temptations?

While I was in college I was involved in a campus ministry that
strongly discouraged dating. The men and women in that minis-

try rarely if ever spent time together outside of the regular group meetings.

One day I talked about this policy with one of the older female students. She spoke in terms of concern for her younger sisters: "It tends to encourage them—especially the baby Christians—to go out with non-Christian guys," she said. "While the non-Christian guys are spending time with them, complimenting them, paying them attention, and asking them out on dates, the Christian guys ignore them."

And she was right. Far too often, the men who should have been blessing these women, the men who, more than anyone else, should have been caring for them—their brothers—wouldn't give them the time of day.

At the time I heard this report, I had a job in my dorm's grill. It so happened that most nights right after dinner four of the guys from the group would come down to the grill and play cards for an hour or two. They'd sit, play cards, and talk.

One night I became indignant. *Why should they spend all their time with one another?* I thought. *Why aren't they caring for their sisters?* I walked over to where they were sitting. "Why don't you guys spend time with your sisters?" I asked. "I've talked with several of the women and they say they never get asked out on dates by Christian men."

"Oh!" one of them answered. "I couldn't go out on a date! I remember my B.C. (Before Christ) days and how I treated girls back then. I don't think I could handle the temptations."

The Danger of Spending Time Alone Together

Jim Talley and Bobbie Reed speak for many counselors when they suggest that there is a virtual cause-and-effect relationship between men and women spending time alone together and their becoming sexually involved. "(We use) an arbitrary but . . . reasonable figure of three hundred hours alone together to show how a relationship develops from acquaintance to a sexually active involvement," they write. "The (development) of the relationship is controlled by the hours spent alone together."[1]

If Talley and Reed are correct, my friend had the right idea. He had to beware of spending time with his sisters—not only because of his past, but because spending time alone together with a member of the opposite sex is inherently dangerous: the more such time you spend, the more sexually active you will become.

"Long time periods alone together discharge our moral batteries," suggest Talley and Reed.[2] Without a recharge, apparently, a couple is sure to fall into sin. Similar to what happens when one uses rechargeable batteries in a flashlight, when spending time alone together with a member of the opposite sex, you can only go so long before you need a moral recharge. Consistent with their battery metaphor, Talley and Reed conclude, "We need time apart to recharge our resistance to immorality."[3]

Scripturally, of course, such a suggestion is ridiculous. Brothers and sisters don't need time apart to recharge their moral batteries! Christians are supposed to *come together* in order to encourage each other and to "spur one another on to love and good deeds" (Hebrews 10:24–25).

"Oh, yes," people reply, "but when you get a red-blooded man together with a warm-bodied woman, you've got to watch out! The problem isn't simply time *together*, it's time *alone* together."

And I am willing to concede the point. There are dangers involved in spending time alone together with members of the opposite sex. The dangers are far greater, however, in some circumstances than in others.

For instance, Talley and Reed point out that as long as people remain friends they can accumulate time alone together and never get caught on the sexual-involvement escalator. "Accumulated time alone together [only] becomes significant as a controlling factor [in moving a couple toward sexual involvement] *when suddenly the couple discover that they are more than friends*" (emphasis added).[4]

And what do Talley and Reed mean by being "more than friends"? "Physical contact is a perfectly natural part" of a "more than friends" relationship, they say, though "most of the time alone together should be spent doing such things as sharing ideas, working on projects, participating in sports, or sharing spiritually."[5] The reason, of course, is that "a whole Saturday spent painting the kitchen together is much less dangerous than several hours spent cuddling and kissing passionately in a darkened room while listening to romantic music."[6] Indeed!

They, obviously, are not talking about a brother-sister relationship!

Brothers and sisters don't "suddenly discover that they are more than friends." They don't let time alone together become a significant controlling factor in their lives. They are not helpless victims of "love" or of their hormones. They control who they become more than friends with. They take responsibility for their relationships. They speak the truth, use no guile, guard their hearts and refuse to make unspoken, unwanted, unmeant, lying vows. They neither speak about nor act upon their commitments until those commitments are well defined. Brothers and sisters don't take physical contact for granted. Physical contact is not just a "perfectly natural part" of their relationship. It's something they engage in for a purpose and with a meaning. An encouraging touch, a welcoming embrace: socially and emotionally affirming contact is fine. Sexual contact is out. Brothers and sisters stay away from "cuddling and kissing passionately"—in darkened rooms or elsewhere.

"But time alone together is still dangerous!"

Yes. And brothers and sisters pay attention to those dangers: not only for their own sake, but for the sake of others as well.

Overcoming the Dangers

"Be careful . . . that the exercise of your freedom does not become a stumbling block to the weak," Paul warns in 1 Corinthians 8:9. He happened to be talking about eating meat sacrificed to idols. The warning is equally valid in relation to spending time alone together with members of the opposite sex. "If what I eat causes my brother to fall into sin, I will never eat meat again, so that I will not cause him to fall," Paul writes (1 Corinthians 8:13). He could have just as easily written, "If spending time alone together with a member of the opposite sex causes my brother or sister to fall into sin, I will never spend time alone together with a member of the opposite sex. . . ."

Brothers and sisters do not relate to one another as they do merely for their own pleasure. They spend time together in order that they might be a blessing: to themselves, to one another, and to the world around them. If their times together will be a curse to any one of those groups, they will refuse to get together . . . or do whatever else they must to overcome the dangers.

Pastors often refuse to counsel women when they are by themselves. They will ask another person, a witness, to be present in the room. Or they will open the door to the outer office. They will do these things not only to avoid the *temptations* of evil but to avoid even the *appearance* of evil.

The Apostle Paul, when entrusted with the job of taking a large gift to the believers at Jerusalem, wrote, "We are taking pains to do what is right, not only in the eyes of the Lord but *also in the eyes of men*" (2 Corinthians 8:21, emphasis added).

Brothers and sisters follow Paul's example. If, to avoid criticism, they must always be in groups, then they will spend their time together in groups. If they must never close the door of a room where they find themselves together, then they will keep the door open.

People ask, "How can you get to know another person, especially get to know them well, if you never spend time alone with them?"

I answer: There are few subjects two people cannot talk about in the middle of a group, while walking down the sidewalk, or while sitting in a room where the door is open and another person could walk in at any time. People are usually happy to give others the kind of privacy they need for intimate conversation. Privacy is not generally something you have to work hard at to create for yourself.

Privacy doesn't require being alone, away from other humans, in a darkened car or locked room. In fact, I know of no situations in non-marriage relationships requiring closed or locked doors, private motel rooms, empty apartments, or lonely spots away from other human beings.

One of my friends once told me he was homosexual. He'd never told another soul before in his life. I believe it was good that when he shared his secret, he told it to me in private. But his revelation required no locked doors, parked car, or dark and lonely spot at the end of a dirt road! Jim and I were out for a walk along a fairly well-lit and well-traveled road. Anyone driving by could have seen what we were doing. They would have had no idea what it was we were talking about, but they could have seen what we were doing. Our privacy was maintained while we remained exposed to public scrutiny. There was no possibility that someone could have charged us with immorality or indecency.

In the same way, brothers and sisters are able to avoid evil and even the appearance of evil. They are happy to be seen in public. They are willing to carry on private conversations in the middle of crowded rooms. They just talk quietly enough that no one is able to listen in without being invited.

But we've drifted from the main point of this chapter. Brothers and sisters spend time together. Lots of time. Different kinds of time. They make time for one another, redeem the time, and always, always, always *live reality*.

Questions for Study and Discussion

1. According to Hebrews 10:24–25, why should Christians want to spend time together?

2. According to Genesis 2:18, why might it be appropriate not only for members of the same sex but for members of the opposite sex—brothers and sisters—to spend time together?

3. At what point(s) and for what reason(s) would it be sinful for you to spend time with one of your brothers or sisters?

4. What are your feelings about the idea that brothers and sisters would (or, as suggested in this chapter, even "should") drop in on one another unannounced and un-planned-for?

5. How do you feel about the suggestions to "make time," "redeem time," and "live reality"?

6. Besides asking each other out on dates, how can brothers and sisters show that they care for one another?

7. Some people (see chapter 10) suggest group dating as a positive alternative to the common practice of men and women dating one-on-one.

   a. What advantages and disadvantages do you see to this proposal? Under what circumstances would group dating offer significant advantages? When could it be detrimental?

   b. Is group dating a foolproof means for avoiding sexual immorality? Why or why not?

   c. How can you best protect yourself from becoming involved in sexual immorality?

8. Talley and Reed say that "accumulated time alone together becomes significant as a controlling factor [in a relationship] *when suddenly the couple discovers that they are more than friends.*"

   a. Does time alone together ever have to become a controlling factor in a relationship? Why or why not?

   b. Couples do often "suddenly discover" something immediately prior or right at the time they begin "going" together. What is it that they discover?

9. Comment on the following statements. (Is the logic correct? Are the assumptions correct? How would *you* respond?)

—If Paul and Rhonda merely *discover* that they are more than friends, then they must already have *been* more than friends before they made the discovery.

—If Paul and Rhonda became more than friends before they made the discovery, then they must have exerted no conscious control over the process that led to their becoming "more than friends."

—If Paul and Rhonda exerted no conscious control over the process that led to their becoming "more than friends," then they neither decided *when* or *with whom* they would enjoy this "more than friends" relationship.

—If Paul and Rhonda decided neither when nor with whom they would enjoy their "more than friends" relationship, they are helpless victims of Fate—or, as songwriters would prefer to express it, potential victims of "Love."

—If Paul and Rhonda are helpless victims of Fate or potential victims of "Love," their "more than friends" relationship could end just as easily as it began—-without their knowledge or control.

10. Are you able to exert control over when or with whom you become "more than friends"?

11. Besides their comment about accumulated time becoming a controlling factor in a relationship *after* a couple discover that they are more than friends, Talley and Reed also say that the hours a couple spend alone together control the development of a relationship *from acquaintanceship*. If there is any truth to these statements, then it must be possible to be "more than friends" yet no more than acquaint-

ances, i.e., to be *more* than friends yet not *even* friends. In what sense can these things be true? Or are they true?

12. What does it mean to be a friend?

13. Do your "moral batteries" get discharged when you are with members of your own sex? Why or why not? Do they get discharged when you are with members of the opposite sex? Why or why not?

14. According to 1 Corinthians 5:9–11, what kind of people are likely to wear down your moral batteries?

If you, then, though you are evil, know how to give good gifts to your children, how much more will your Father in heaven give good gifts to those who ask him!

Matthew 7:11

He who did not spare his own Son, but gave him up for us all— how will he not also, along with him, graciously give us all things?

Romans 8:32

9

NO GRIEVOUS BURDEN

Brothers and Sisters Trust God to Meet Their Needs and Fulfill Their Hearts' Desires

I n the course of the average year, few churches in the United States are likely to say much about the fourth commandment: "Remember the Sabbath day by keeping it holy. Six days you shall labor and do all your work, but the seventh day is a Sabbath to the LORD your God. On it you shall not do any work, neither you, nor your son or daughter, nor your manservant or maidservant, nor your animals, nor the alien within your gates" (Exodus 20:8–10; also Deuteronomy 5:12–15).

I certainly grew up without ever having heard a sermon on the topic. Indeed, as far as my life was concerned, the Sabbath didn't exist. I grew up in evangelical, "Bible-believing" circles, yet I never knew any Christians who "remembered" the Sabbath and "kept it holy" by refraining from work. Yet somehow, I know, I was familiar with the command. And the few times I ever thought about it, I rebelled at the idea.

How mean God is! I thought. *He tells us we can only work six days a week! What gall! He wants to take away the one day each week in which I can catch up on all my work!* Not only that, but, I thought, *He attaches the death penalty to this awful command* (see Exodus 35:2). *How cruel can one get?*

The thought never crossed my mind that He was actually being gracious.

Commandments as Blessing

Late in high school I ran across a book called *Ten Great Freedoms* by Ernst Lange. Lange put the Ten Commandments in a different perspective. His handling of the fourth commandment, in particular, was striking. Speaking as with the voice of God, Lange said, "You don't need to run yourself to death! . . . I, the almighty God, want to be your master. Hold onto me, and your life will find fulfillment."[1]

Suddenly I realized that the fourth commandment—as, indeed, all God's commands—is not a legalistic, burdensome requirement. Rather, it is a commandment of faith: if I will only trust God, I will find His commandments give me release, joyous *relief* from the harsh demands of my illegitimate masters, sin and Satan.

"Come to me, all you who are weary and burdened, and I will give you rest. Take my yoke upon you and learn from me, for I am gentle and humble in heart, and you will find rest for your souls. For my yoke is easy and my burden is light," Jesus said (Matthew 11:28–30).

Instead of fifty-two days a year of awful duty, in the fourth commandment God was offering me—no, commanding me, *requiring* me—to take fifty-two days a year of vacation. And He was so serious about this requirement that, when He gave the decree, He told His people, "If you disobey, you're going to die!"

The sabbath commandment took on a different shine for me. Beginning in my sophomore year at college, I decided to take God at His word. Now while all my neighbors are grunting, groaning, and working themselves to death with a non-stop, seven-day-a-week work schedule, I enjoy a weekly vacation. I look forward to Sundays as a day to sleep in (till 7:00; normally I'm up at 4:30) and a day to enjoy deep fellowship with friends at church. It's the day on which I get to take a nap, relax, read a book—do all the things I can't do when I'm hurrying and scurrying about my daily activities. It's a day, beyond all else, when I am able to enjoy relationships and rejuvenate my mind, body, and spirit.

Is the sabbath commandment a loathsome burden to me? By no means! It is something I treasure most highly.

The same shift in perspective and attitude can come about when we consider the principles and commandments concerning brother-sister relationships. We can look at these things from the perspective that God is a killjoy: "I don't want you to have fun with members of the opposite sex. I don't want you to get involved in any physical-sexual intimacy."

Or we can look at them from another perspective. God wants only the best for us: "Why entangle yourself in false vows and promises? Why open yourself to the pain and hurt of betrayed trust? Why, indeed, should you enjoy anything less than the full freedom I have given you? Don't limit yourself to enjoying mental, emotional, and spiritual intimacy with only one member of the opposite sex! Enjoy yourself! Enjoy your brothers and sisters! Bless and *be* blessed. Save yourself from commitments until you're ready to fulfill them, and refrain from limiting your relations until you know that such limitations will help you do My will!" Is there anything more beautiful than that?

God calls us to faith. He calls us to obedience. "Trust Me," He says. "I know a better way."

Trusting God to Meet Needs and Fulfill Desires

I find it interesting that we never read of Adam falling on his face and pleading with God to "just give me a wife!" God seems to have recognized Adam's need long before Adam was ever aware of it. It was God, not Adam, who said, "It is not good for the man to be alone" (Genesis 2:18). It was God, not Adam, who recognized Adam's need for "a helper suitable for him."

While I was in college and treating my sisters in the Lord as I would my biological sisters, there were several women with whom I "fell in love." They were very special to me: physically beautiful, intellectually stimulating. . . . I was powerfully and romantically attracted to them.

I'll admit it was difficult for me to refrain from engaging in the kinds of behavior—the unspoken vows and promises, the physical-sexual intimacy, the ownership and obligation—that we've been saying brothers and sisters avoid. I wanted to enjoy the pleasure of "having and holding" a woman. I wanted to own her and have the pleasure of physical-sexual intimacy with her. I wanted the sense of security, the comfort, the pleasure that such intimacy can bring.

But I also knew that I was unprepared to pay the price and had no interest in the responsibility and obligation those privileges entail.

And so I waited. And watched. One sister moved away. Another abandoned the brother-sister model to pursue a boyfriend-girlfriend relationship.

Was I losing out? Once a sister abandoned the brother-sister model to go with someone else, I knew I would rarely spend the time together with her that we had once enjoyed. Our intense conversations were almost surely a thing of the past. So, yes, I felt the loss. I felt it keenly. Moreover, I wondered: Was I ever going to get married?

Still, having avoided the bonds of false vows and promises, having refused to let my heart be stirred by physical-sexual intimacy, having abstained from a false sense of ownership, I knew when my sisters left me that I was experiencing nowhere near the pain I would have experienced had I allowed myself to enjoy these illicit luxuries.

Every time one of these special sisters moved on, I found myself remarking to God: "Oh, Lord! If not her, then who? She was so wonderful! I can't imagine someone being better than her."

And then I'd think again and ask, "Is it possible that You have chosen someone even better for me?"

"[If God] did not spare his own Son, but gave him up for us all—how will he not also, along with him, graciously give us all things?" Paul asks in Romans 8:32. You know the answer to that question as well as I do. We are taught to respond—joyfully, resoundingly, with faith: "Yes! Of course! God will graciously give us *all* things."

"Every good and perfect gift is from above, coming down from the Father of the heavenly lights," James tells us (James 1:17).

Jesus exclaims in Matthew 7:11: "If you, then, though you are evil, know how to give good gifts to your children, how much more will your Father in heaven give good gifts to those who ask him!" And Paul echoes with the words: God is "able to do immeasurably more than all we ask or imagine" (Ephesians 3:20).

And God *is* able! And He *does* far more than all we ask or imagine. He has done it in my case and He can do it in yours, too.

The question I had to answer, and the question you must answer is, "Will I trust God to do what He has promised? Will I obey His word? Will I do what He tells me and believe Him when He says He means it for my good (see Romans 8:28)?"

Brothers and sisters obey God's commandments because they trust Him to meet their needs and to fulfill their hearts' desires.

Questions for Study and Discussion

1. What do you find hardest to trust God for as you consider the possibility of pursuing brother-sister relationships?

2. Is there any reason you would like to ignore the brother-sister model and pursue the kinds of relationships that are standard in our culture—boyfriend-girlfriend and "serious" relationships, for instance?

    a. What are you afraid you would miss if you were to obey God in the area of brother-sister relationships?

    b. By *disobeying* God, would you have any more likelihood of acquiring the things you're afraid you'll miss? Why or why not?

3. Is there any reason you would like to pursue the brother-sister model and avoid the kinds of relationships that are standard in our culture?

    a. What are you afraid you would miss if you were to disobey God in the area of brother-sister relationships?

    b. By *obeying* God, would you have any more likelihood of acquiring the things you're afraid you'll miss? Why or why not?

4. Good marriages are based on trust, among other things.

    a. What are some ways that a boyfriend-girlfriend relationship might help you to test another person's trustworthiness better than a brother-sister relationship could?

    b. How about ways a brother-sister relationship might be superior to a boyfriend-girlfriend relationship in helping you test another person's trustworthiness?

5. Compare brother-sister and boyfriend-girlfriend relationships. How may each be better than the other in helping you establish a good marriage?

6. According to 2 Samuel 12:14 and other portions of Scripture (see Ephesians 4:27, 30; James. 4:7; 1 Peter 5:8; Job 1:8; 2:3; 1 Samuel 17:45–47; etc.): how important is it that you obey God and that you keep away from sin? What are some of the consequences for sin, on the one hand, and obedience on the other?

7. In *Beating the Break-Up Habit*,[2] Dick Purnell says he believes there are five major reasons boyfriend-girlfriend re-

lationships die. If participants could just overcome these difficulties, he says, they would "beat the break-up habit"; they would be able to stick together. The five major problems Purnell lists are in the areas of:

1. Communication (dishonesty, lack of openness)

2. Expectations (having unrealistic expectations about the relationship)

3. Response to partner's expectations (having such a low self-image that one does everything to please his or her partner)

4. Motivation (selfishness)

5. Sexual involvement (too much, too fast, too soon leads to "burnout")

a. How can unspoken, unwanted, unmeant, unintentional vows or promises affect a couple's *openness and honesty* with one another? Would such vows help or hinder openness and honesty?

b. How can unspoken, unwanted, unmeant, unintentional vows or promises affect a couple's *expectations* concerning the relationship?

c. Purnell suggests that it is a person's low self-image that will lead to inappropriate responses to one's partner's expectations. Describe how a sense of obligation—feeling as if one is owned—could also contribute to such poor responses.

d. For what reasons might a person want to make an unspoken, unwanted, unmeant, unintentional vow or promise to another? Are any of these reasons *un*selfish? Explain.

e. Based on your own experience, what you have read in this book, and your answers to questions (a) through (d) above, do you think it is ever possible for boy-

friends and girlfriends to completely avoid all the problems Purnell mentions? Why or why not?

f. How about brothers and sisters: can they escape these
problems? Why or why not?

8. Add at least two items to each of the following lists of
ways a boyfriend-girlfriend or "serious" dating relationship could neutralize your ability to fulfill your purpose as
a servant of God. ("Brothers and sisters remember their
purpose: to bless.") If you can think of appropriate Scripture passages to go along with what you say, mention
those, too. How could a boyfriend-girlfriend or "serious"
dating relationship neutralize your effectiveness as God's
servant:

a. Before you start "going" together?

- By getting me all wrapped up in concern over
  whether or not I can get someone to become interested in me. (Self-interest rather than other-interest,
  therefore focusing on the blessings I get rather than
  the blessings I give. See 1 Corinthians 13:5;
  Philippians 2:3ff.)

- By getting me to treat some people so much better
  than others that I don't care for the others at all.
  (Same thing as above: that's not very loving! See
  James 2:1–4.)

b. At the moment you start "going" together?

- By getting me to pretend a lie; by getting me to say
  things I don't really mean or couldn't do if I did
  mean them. (Therefore, hurting people in the process.)

c. In the middle of the relationship?

- By getting me to clam up about who I really am,
  and not be totally honest; by getting me to put on a

show for the person I'm trying to impress (my dating partner). (If I'm being dishonest, it means I am not showing God's glory in who I am. So I'm less effective than I ought to be. See Matthew 5:33–37; 2 Corinthians 3:1–3; Ephesians 4:15.)

- By getting me to worry about whether or not my boyfriend (girlfriend) and I will "make it," whether or not our relationship will work out the way I want it to. "Do not be anxious about anything, but in everything . . . present your requests to God" Philippians 4:6–7.

- By having me waste a lot of time and emotional energy trying to make the relationship work. Whereas if I weren't going with this other person, then I wouldn't be spending the time and energy.

- By cutting me off from relationships with other brothers and sisters to whom I might be a blessing or who might be a blessing to me.

d. At the end of the relationship?

- By paralyzing me with grief and pain.
- By loading me down with guilt for having broken the vows or promises I made.

e. After the relationship?

- Since my trust has been betrayed, my ability to trust other people is destroyed.
- By turning me bitter. (See Hebrews 12:15.)
- By ending the relationship with me getting married before I should, or to someone whom I really shouldn't marry—a non-Christian, perhaps, or someone with a totally different life calling from my own. (See 2 Corinthians 6:14ff.)

f. At any other time or in any other way?

- By "yoking" me to someone who is going to drag me down or pull me off the main track God wants me to follow. (Hebrews 12:1)

9. Make a similar list for brother-sister relationships. How could a brother-sister relationship neutralize your effectiveness as God's servant?

10. In the Introduction, Brother-sister relationships are a "gracious gift from a loving God."

   a. In what sense is this true? Can you see any benefits to treating your brothers and sisters in Christ as brothers and sisters?

   b. In what sense could you say the same things about boyfriend-girlfriend or "serious" relationships? Are they gracious gifts from God? What benefits will you gain if you follow our culture's dating pattern?

11. In the Introduction, Brother-sister relationships allow us to "avoid some of the most treacherous ambushes Satan has ever devised for destroying God's people." Do you think that is an overstatement? Why or why not?

12. Write a statement concerning the standards you intend to maintain in your relationships with members of the opposite sex.

13. Why might it be good for you to talk about this document (question 12) with other brothers and sisters? How could they help you live up to those standards?

PART TWO

QUESTIONS AND ANSWERS

10

HOW DO BROTHERS AND SISTERS DATE?

QUESTION: I'm confused. On the one hand you say we're supposed to treat our brothers and sisters in the Lord as if they were our biological brothers and sisters. On the other hand you seem to think it's okay for brothers and sisters in the Lord to date. I wouldn't go out on a date with my natural-born brother. How do you put those things together?

ANSWER: Sarita and I have a friendly disagreement on this subject. She says we never dated until the day we were engaged. I think we dated a lot. I think it really depends on your definition of the word *date*.

I've had friends who, when they've set a time to get together with someone, will say, "It's a *date*." Another way these people may say the same thing is, "Okay. You're *on*," or, "You're on my schedule." You could also say, "We've got a date set," or, "I plan to meet with you at that time." In this sense, a date is merely a preplanned meeting.

Now if that definition of a date is too loose—if, as far as you're concerned, a date is not a date unless it includes a special invitation, getting dressed up, going out somewhere, spending money, setting aside time for physical-sexual intimacy—well, then brothers and sisters—whether spiritual or biological—don't date.

By definition, of course, physical-sexual intimacy is never allowed in a brother-sister relationship. As for the other practices—special invitations, getting dressed up, going out, spending money, whatever—while they're quite all right, they're not necessary. I may invite my friends—or my physical brother 'or sister—to a special event. We may get dressed up, leave our houses, and spend money. On the other hand, we may do none of these things.

As far as I'm concerned, brother-sister dates merely require that you arrange to meet together and then, once you're in each other's presence, you share as many blessings as you can within the limits God has established for brother-sister relationships.

If you're comfortable with that definition of what it means to go on a date, then I would say brothers and sisters date. I dated a lot by that standard. If you don't like that definition, then maybe brothers and sisters don't date.

Brothers and sisters certainly *don't* get together in order to stimulate each other's sexual urges or to induce each other to have a sense of mutual obligation or dependency. They don't meet in order to "prove" they love each other. They don't do anything in order to prove themselves. They get together to bless each other and to build each other up.

ta ta ta

QUESTION: What about dat*ing* or "going together"?

ANSWER: I think you already know my answer. *Dating* in that sense, or *going together*, requires some form of obligation that brothers and sisters avoid. Going out on many dates together: fine. Being *obligated* to go out on dates: forget it.

ta ta ta

QUESTION: So what do brothers and sisters do on dates?

ANSWER: Brothers and sisters can do anything regular friends do. I mentioned a several ideas in chapters 2 and 8 as a way of breaking you out of the stereotypical mold of what you should do on a date. I mentioned what I suggested to Robbie and Kevin, that they might invite some women to go to the auto parts store with them or that they might go along with their sisters as their sisters went grocery shopping. I mentioned inviting Mary to go with me to the car wash.

You can do almost anything with your brother or sister. You can have fun together: work, study, clean your apartment, do laundry, read a book, take a hike, bake some cookies, counsel a friend, write a letter to the editor concerning some issue(s) you feel strongly about. . . . Josh McDowell, in his book, *Givers, Takers and Other Kinds of Lovers* (Tyndale House Publishers, 1980, 102-104), lists many ideas. Most books on dating suggest ideas.

Brothers and sisters can do anything together—except the things I've mentioned brothers and sisters always seek to avoid. Brothers and sisters don't get involved in false vows; they don't place each other in positions of obligation; they don't engage in sexual intimacy. Beyond these few limitations, brothers and sisters are absolutely free.

A lot of people think brother-sister dates as I've described them must be unromantic and boring. "Go shopping together? Help out together in the nursery at church? You've got to be kidding! That's no date!"

I think that instead of holding these kinds of activities in contempt as something you do only after you and your sister (or wife) are fifty years old, bored with each other, and "unable to do anything better," why not face the realities of life and recognize that this is a pattern of dating you can *maintain* for the rest of your life! Why not discover and practice now, while you have no marriage commitments, how to make ordinary events in life useful for maintaining and developing relationships? If you wait until you're married, won't it be too late?

Now is the time to practice life habits. Now is the time to learn how to make even ordinary circumstances extraordinary. Now is the time to learn how to relate to other people—even your future husband or wife—in ways that make sense over the long haul in terms of the kind of time and money you can afford to devote to each other.

Do extraordinary things, too, of course. But work at making ordinary times work for you!

᙭ ᙭ ᙭

QUESTION: Could you comment on movie dates and things like that?

ANSWER: I can't imagine any worse place to get to know another person than at a movie.

Most movie dates I'm familiar with have nothing to do with thoughtfulness, meditation, or communication. They have everything to do with personal entertainment and, usually, physical-sexual intimacy. As such, they are of little use to brothers and sisters who are trying to get to know each other.

TV dates are much the same.

How much intelligent conversation do you normally engage in while the TV is on? I think TV may be implicated in the breakup of many marriages. While the TV is on, people don't talk. At worst, their attention is arrested by the TV. At best, the TV creates an unnecessary distraction to the more important matter of your interpersonal communication.

If you're with an old friend whom you know very well, nothing much is lost if you sit around once in a while watching the TV or a movie. But if you're with someone you're trying to get to know or if habitual TV-watching blocks communication, you're in trouble!

Have you ever wondered why, if you're with a member of the opposite sex, there is such a strong desire in the middle of a movie or in the middle of a TV program to put your arm around her, to hold her hand, or in some other way to become physically involved with her? I've come to the conclusion it has something to do with the fact that without physical contact, there's very little in a TV or movie date that can even remotely be described as intimate.

Without hand-holding, hugging, or some other form of physical intimacy, a movie or TV program simply gives you the opportunity to have your personal experience while the person sitting next to you has his or hers. Your primary interaction is not with the person who's sitting next to you, but with the movie or TV program. And the only way you can overcome your guilt for ignoring this person you're supposed to be getting to know is to try to show you "really are interested" in her, even though you're preoccupied.

My attitude toward movies and TV programs isn't totally negative. If you go to a movie with the idea that you're going to have a discussion afterward, if you know the movie is supposed to be particularly powerful and you plan to use it as a jumping-off point for some heart-to-heart discussion, a movie could be a very useful part of a date. Having the shared experience of watching the movie and then talking it through may be useful in helping the two or more of you get to know each other better. Sometimes a movie can spur a discussion about personal values or social issues you would never otherwise discuss.

🖙 🖙 🖙

QUESTION: What about eating out?

ANSWER: I've already indicated that brothers and sisters may eat out together. But they don't do it in order to impress each other or to create a sense of obligation.

Sarita and I find that when we are in a restaurant where we have nothing else to do but talk and eat, we're better able to communicate than if we're at home with a hundred distractions . . . such as four kids! For that reason, we'll go out to a restaurant.

But eating out is relatively expensive. If money is a problem, then you need to come up with better ways to "get alone" than having to eat in a restaurant.

Sarita and I did a lot of walking when we dated. One evening we sat and read stories. If I were to date now, I think I might go to the library and pick up a copy of *The Cat in the Hat* or some other children's book and do a dramatic reading. Kids' books can be great fun! (Try a James Stevenson, Steven Kellogg, Bill Peet, or James Marshall book, or Dorothy Weinmann Sharmat's *Nate the Great* series. There are dozens of creative authors to choose from.)

There are so many things to do with friends, so many useful, good, productive things: Don't fall into the mold of the world that would have you sit back passively to be entertained.

ఎ ఎ ఎ

QUESTION: There's a girl I would like to get to know. We've never talked, but she goes to my church so I see her each week. She seems really nice. Do you have any suggestions on how I can begin a brother-sister relationship with her?

ANSWER: Assuming you're both Christians, you're already her brother. What you need to do is develop a friendship with her. So how do you do that?

From what I've seen, friendships usually begin when outside circumstances throw two people together in the midst of a group. The soon-to-be friends discover within the context of a group that they have mutual interests. Having made that discovery, they then decide to team up and pursue their interests further on their own. After a while as the relationship grows, trust builds and understanding develops; they become friends.

If I wanted to develop a friendship with a girl and I knew of no mutual interest that would naturally throw us together, I would find or create some group activities in which we might have a common interest and in which conversation between us could take place easily.

Your church, obviously, is something in which you and this young woman both have an interest. But apparently your church is not creating a climate in which you're being encouraged to speak with her. You probably need a smaller group for that.

I recommend that you find or form a group of four to six people—definitely no more than a dozen—in which you and your sister will virtually have to speak to one another, yet in which neither you nor she will be under pressure to continue conversing one with the other.

If the two of you together compose one-third to half the group, how can you help but meet and speak to each other? At the same time, though you'll be forced to address each other, neither of you will have to worry about keeping the conversation going all by yourselves.

Unlike a one-on-one dating situation in which it's all up to you and your sister whether or not you have a good time, when you're with a group of friends, neither of you has to worry about the other person being a boor or a bore or a less than pleasurable companion.

From what you've told me, at this point you don't know how your sister thinks or where her interests lie. What if her interests are totally different from yours? What if her sense of humor is different? If you are on a one-on-one date and you don't hit it off just right, you could be in for a very long and uncomfortable evening!

That's the advantage of a group. It can free you from these pressures. Whether you're shy or outgoing, rich or poor, highly refined or still a bit rough around the edges, the group will give you and your sister room to grow. If your sister likes you the way you are, well, that's fine! If she doesn't, that's fine, too. You'll both soon discover whether or not you want to spend time together in a more intense, one-on-one context.

〜　〜　〜

QUESTION: Could you say a little more about the kinds of things we might do with a group? And what about the invitation? If you were in my shoes, how would you go about inviting her?

ANSWER: By *group* activities I mean activities in which both you and your sister are equally members and guests—not of each other, but of the group. If you invite her (and it's possible someone else would be better suited to do that than you), your invitation should go something like, "Hi, Sherri! A bunch of us are going down to the beach tomorrow. We're wondering if you'd like to come along."

Notice I said, *we*: "*We* were wondering," not, "*I* was wondering." Sherri should not be *your* guest; she should be the guest of the group.

At the beginning of your relationship, especially, the dangers of placing a person in a position of obligation are great. You need to avoid anything that will suggest to Sherri that you are trying to obligate her to you.

That's another reason you should avoid one-on-one dates at the beginning of a relationship. Until you know and trust each other thoroughly as friends, you should avoid any activities or situations in which you and she might be looked upon as a couple or in which she considers herself to be your guest.

However you phrase your invitation, the primary question Sherri should have to answer is, "Do I want to go to the beach?" not, "Do I want to spend a day with John?" There is no reason she should have to make a decision that has overtones of accepting or rejecting you when she hardly knows who you are!

ta ta ta

QUESTION: How about answering the same kinds of questions for us girls? There are times when we would like to get to know guys, but we can't just walk up to them and ask them out.

ANSWER: And why not?

QUESTION: That would be weird!

ANSWER: What's weird about a sister asking her brother to come along on a group activity? If you make it clear to him that you're a part of a group that's going to do something and that you all would like him to join you, there's nothing weird about that.

Again, consistency is the key. If you're consistent in your behavior, if you're truly friends to all your brothers and sisters, and especially if you're asking in the context of a group activity, there should be absolutely no problem with your calling on a guy to invite him out for a date.

ẽ ẽ ẽ

QUESTION: Do you have any other comments you would like to make about group dating?

ANSWER: First, I would like to stress the ministry possibilities.

In almost every group—high school, college, singles, adults, *every* group—there is at least one person who is painfully, awkwardly, clumsily, boorishly shy; someone who is on the outside looking in. As a loving brother or sister in the Lord, you will want to minister to that person, helping him to feel accepted, helping him to "join the real world." But you may not want to shoulder that burden all by yourself. Group dates can ease the situation. They can free you and the rest of your group to minister to social outcasts without finding yourselves smothered in an overwhelmingly needy embrace.

And, if I hardly knew a person, man or woman, I would rather get to know him or her in the relative safety of a group than find myself in the passenger seat of a car while George is driving drunk or in the driver's seat while Geraldine is making passes at me.

"Aw-w-w, come on!" George may chide when I tell him I would rather go slow and get to know him first in group contexts. "What's the matter? Don't you trust me?"

"No, I don't trust you!" I would respond. "I have no reason to trust you. I have no reason *not* to trust you, but I don't have an adequate reason *to* trust you, either. I know what you're like in Chemistry class, but I would prefer to know you better in other contexts before going out with you alone."

"Children: don't go with strangers," the posters and television commercials used to say. There is wisdom in that slogan. There's wisdom in that slogan for daters, too. "Daters: don't go with strangers."

Why? A stranger is a person whose character qualities you have been unable to evaluate adequately. A stranger may be a charmer, or he may be a social dud. He may be very kind and well intentioned, or he may be very evil. George may seem nice enough at the office or in Chemistry 101, but once you observe him on his own or in the presence of friends, you may find he likes traveling the fast lane. Maybe he's rebellious toward his parents, or he's into drugs or alcohol. Maybe once you go out with him, you'll find he is all passion and self-centeredness. According to an article in *Campus Life* magazine,[1] date abuse occurs in as many as 50 percent of all relationships!

(By the way, if you're a parent and you are concerned about the safety of your child or the character of the kids he or she is running around with, you have every right to intervene and say you don't want him or her associating with a particular person or crowd until you've gotten to know them better. The trust factor is just as important between you and your children as it is between them and any potential dating partners. Lack of trust doesn't necessarily mean *mis*trust or *dis*trust. It can mean nothing more than, "I don't have adequate information to form an opinion.")

QUESTION: So how long do you think a relationship needs to stay at the "group" level before progressing to one-on-one?

ANSWER: Simply stated, you shouldn't date a person one-on-one until you're no longer strangers. That means, at minimum, you will have had at least one significant, in-depth conversation with the person you're considering.

⁙ ⁙ ⁙

QUESTION: Okay. I'm fifteen, and I know this guy—we're definitely not strangers—but my parents won't let me go out with him. They say I'm not old enough. What do you think? How old do you have to be before you date?

ANSWER: I think age has very little to do with the answer to your question. You may be fifteen and not ready to date, or you may be thirty-five and not ready to date. I think the following guidelines are more important than age when it comes to being prepared *within yourself* for one-on-one dating.

You will be ready to date one-on-one when you have acquired:

1. A clearly established purpose for spending time with a member of the opposite sex. In other words, you, your parents, and any other interested parties (that means anyone who has a legitimate interest in your well-being, including, I hope, the person you want to go out with) should have a means of evaluating each date: what was good about it, what was bad, what you will want to do in the future to improve your success, etc.

2. Carefully thought-out convictions about how you ought to conduct yourself in relation to members of the opposite sex.

3. An understanding of why you ought to relate to your brothers and sisters in the way you have decided to relate to them.

4. An ability to explain your convictions to another person.

5. The desire and internal strength necessary to express your convictions and make them stick when someone opposes you.

Until you meet all these criteria, you are not ready to date one-on-one.

If you don't know why you want to date guys, any guys, or if you don't know why you *don't* want to date certain guys (non-Christians, for instance), you have no business going out.

You need to find out why you believe what you believe and you need to decide whether you want to obey God or run your life your own way.

Some Christian leaders suggest girls should rely on their parents to provide the excuse they need to turn down non-Christian guys' invitations to go out with them. I think if you can't turn down a non-Christian's invitation, you have no business going out with anyone. You obviously lack the internal strength necessary to stand up for your own convictions. And since you're the only one who can stand up for your convictions when you're alone on a one-on-one date, you're putting yourself in extreme danger if you go out by yourself and lack that kind of fortitude.

Until you are willing and able to express your convictions in a way that a guy, Christian or non-Christian, can understand and is willing to accept, you shouldn't be out alone.

One final comment on this matter. The right to date alone, one-on-one, is not a worthy goal for brothers and sisters to pursue. Brothers and sisters don't pursue one-on-one time with each other as if spending such time together is a valid and useful goal *in itself*. Physical brothers and sisters don't do that; friends don't do it; brothers and sisters in the Lord don't do it either.

Of course brothers and sisters, both physical and spiritual, spend time together one-on-one, but the focus of that time is usually some mutual interest *outside* their relationship, not the prospect of bonding themselves together more closely. If you're pursuing a one-on-one relationship for its own sake, you're looking for trouble.

Brothers and sisters don't "achieve" one-on-one. They simply spend time together by themselves if it makes sense for them to do so. Remember: brothers and sisters remember their purpose! Their purpose is not particularly to give themselves pleasure; their purpose is to bless and build up one another and other people beyond the bounds of their relationship. One of the ways you and your brothers and sisters can bless each other is by getting to know one another. But you don't need to spend time alone, one-on-one, in order to do that.

⡺ ⡺ ⡺

QUESTION: So are you saying we should never spend time alone with one another? You seem to come down pretty hard on that in chapter 8.

ANSWER: No. I think spending time alone with another person is fine . . . if it's in the right context. In chapter 8, I was giving some of the "rules" for a right context, and some of those "rules" are tough.

My biggest concern is not whether people are by themselves or in the midst of large groups. My concern is that brothers and sisters get to know each other. And the way two people get to know each other is by listening, talking and listening. . . . About in that order.

James said that we should all be "quick to listen [and] slow to speak" (James 1:19). I think he had the order right.

As I tried to prove in chapter 8, getting to know another person doesn't require a lot of being by yourselves alone. Brothers and sisters may spend time alone together, but they don't spend that time alone together "simply" so they can be alone. They spend that time alone together because it's okay to be together alone: they have valid objectives that draw them together—valid objectives *outside of the objective of being alone.*

If your relationship with one of your sisters develops long enough, you'll find that you spend time alone together not so much because the two of you have planned it that way ("At last! We get to be together alone!"), but because such time comes naturally. You won't be particularly thinking about it; it will simply "happen." You and your sister will find that, in the middle of larger groups, you naturally tend to talk with one another. You won't have to go out of your way in order to make those conversations happen. You'll simply find that both of you tend to gravitate together. You'll like spending time together. The two of you will like how the other thinks. You'll appreciate each other's opinions. And so you'll seek each other out. At some point one of you will realize, *Boy! We've got to get together more often! This 'habit' of ours of meeting only once a month (or once every other week, just when there's a party . . . or whatever) is not enough.* And so you'll ask your sister, "Can we get together again to talk about this subject some more?"

Thus, in the midst of a friendship—a relationship based on knowledge, affection and trust, a relationship first developed in group contexts—you'll find yourselves spending time alone together. But the reasons for your meeting one-on-one won't be to entangle each other in a web of romantic deceit, in physical-sexual intimacy, or other forms of behavior that brothers and sisters studiously avoid. It will be to pursue conversations and activities of mutual interest—conversations and activities of mutual interest generally *outside* the relationship itself.

ta   ta   ta

QUESTION: I hate being a stick-in-the-mud, but I just have a problem with your recommending we should ever spend time alone together with members of the opposite sex. There are simply too many temptations.

ANSWER: I'm glad you're aware of the possibility of being tempted. Having recognized it, however, you need to step out and overcome it.

There are a lot of dangers in spending time alone together with members of the opposite sex. But you know something? I think you're faced with no fewer temptations when you and a special woman are in the company of others. The dangers you face aren't created by your circumstances, *they're created by you.*

If you choose to be dishonest with your sister (or she with you), if you choose to lead each other on, if you choose to pursue a course of sensuality and impurity or to do any of a hundred different things that are beneath God's best, other people won't stop you. No friends nearby will be able to stop you.

The presence of friends may discourage you from engaging in sexual intercourse or heavy petting, but it won't keep you from committing the "sin before the sin," the sin that's at the root of all boyfriend-girlfriend and so-called "serious" dating relationships: the dishonest vows, the implying to each other that you've made a greater commitment to one another than you really have.

Ultimately, you and your sisters are the ones who will have to protect yourselves from the entanglements of false vows and false communication. And you'll have to do those things on your own. No friends are going to be able to help you. You'll have to make a firm decision that whether you're in the company of others or not, you will maintain your integrity before your sisters and speak and act truthfully. Period. No matter what.

ᵃ ᵃ ᵃ

QUESTION: You've said that you and Sarita remained just friends or "brother-sister" until the day you were engaged. I have a very hard time believing that. How could you have come to the point where you knew you wanted to marry without having centered in and become exclusive in your relationship? You must have focused! I can't believe you didn't limit each other's contacts with other members of the opposite sex.

ANSWER: It is true that we spent more time together toward the end of our pre-engagement relationship than we did when we first met. But we didn't exclude other people from our conversations or try to keep them from joining us. For instance, we didn't sit by ourselves so other people felt as if they were intruding if they wanted to join us. I don't think we ever ate lunch by ourselves. We always sat with a group. Now it so happened that after an hour and a half, the other people we ate with were all talked out, while Sarita and I still had more to discuss. But if someone had wanted to stick around and join us, we would have been delighted to have them stay. And that would have held true as much at the end of our pre-engagement relationship as at the beginning.

QUESTION: But what about as far as dating is concerned? Didn't you limit your dating to one another? I mean, if one of you had dated someone else, wouldn't you have been at least a little jealous? Come on! Be honest! If Sarita had gone out with someone else, you would have been at least a little offended, wouldn't you?

ANSWER: A friend of ours asked this very question of us one day as he, Sarita, and I sat around our kitchen table. Sarita and I both chuckled as we remembered some of the things we'd done only days before we got engaged.

"Before John asked me to marry him," Sarita told Kevin, "I had no idea where our relationship was going to go. I actually thought we might remain brother-sister forever. So the weekend before we got engaged, I went out on a date with another guy. I had a great time with him. In fact, I was planning to go out with him again. He was upset when three weeks later, he found out I was engaged. He thought I had deliberately led him on, made him think I was unattached when actually I was. Of course he was mistaken!"

I told Kevin about my fiasco with Sally and Carrie. (See chapter 5.)

The point is that, no, there is no need for jealousy. In Sarita's and my relationship there was no *room* for jealousy. We both knew we had no rights of ownership over the other. Sarita had no obligation to me; I had no obligation to her. We could spend as much or as little time with anyone we wanted, including one another. And yet, despite—or, rather, *because of* that freedom, we were able to get to know each other well. We knew each other at least as well as any other pre-engaged couples I've met, and better than most.

The fact that Sarita and I were free to date other people had no negative impact on our ability to get to know each other. If anything, it meant we came to understand each other better than we would have otherwise. Because we had no obligations to limit our interaction with others and because we recognized our obligation before the Lord to be honest with one another, if Sarita had fallen in love with another guy, while she would have had no obligation necessarily to tell me about it, she would have had no reason *not* to tell me about it. Further, she would have been under obligation before the Lord not to cover it over (see chapter 3). Similarly for me. When I was "in love" with other girls, Sarita knew about it. And we talked about it.

The fact that we could know these things about each other meant that we were better able to observe exactly what it was we were looking for in marriage partners, and therefore, when the time came, were better prepared to marry one another.

⋅⋅⋅ ⋅⋅⋅ ⋅⋅⋅

QUESTION: Did you ever tell Sarita you loved her before you got engaged?

ANSWER: Not in so many words. I'm sure I signed some letters, "Love, Your Brother John." But I made sure she knew the love of which I was speaking was brotherly love, not the kind of love of which so-called lovers speak when they say they love each other.

QUESTION: But how could she be sure of your love if you came in on her from nowhere: no statements of love, no signs of love, no physical affection, no hugging, no kissing? If I had been in her shoes, I don't think I would have believed you!

ANSWER: Oh, but you would have! No question about it. You would have known that I was a man of integrity who refused to say what I didn't mean. You would have known the kind of pressures I had been under and the pressures I had *resisted* to tell you I loved you before I was sure I meant what I was saying.

If you were like Sarita and had any interest in marrying me, I'm sure you would have indicated that. "But," I would have told you (as, in fact, I told Sarita), "much as I might like to marry you—and, indeed, I have a lot of feelings in that direction—I am not prepared to make the kinds of commitments to you that marriage would require. And so I'm not going to 'string you along.' I'm not going to play games with you. I'm not going to say I love you until I'm sure that's what I mean."

QUESTION: But using your illustration (supposing I'm Sarita), you just said you *do* love me, you *did* love me, a long time before you ever asked me to marry you! You said you had a lot of feelings in the direction of marriage. What does that mean except love?

ANSWER: It means I had a lot of mushy, gushy feelings. So what?

What is love? Isn't love supposed to be forever? That's what the Bible says. Real love doesn't end (see 1 Corinthians 13:8). It keeps on going even when the other person is unlovable or unlovely. Brother-sister love is like that. Jesus told us to treat all of our brothers and sisters the same way, with the same kind of *agape* love with which He loved us.

But now you're upset because I didn't tell Sarita I loved her in a special way beyond that brother-sister kind of love. You wish I had told her I had special feelings toward her. As I pointed out in chapter 5, feelings don't count; commitment does.

I'm convinced if I'd told Sarita I loved her in that special way "beyond brother-sister," I would have been implying to her that I loved her as a husband is supposed to love his wife. Only I would have been telling her these things *before I was convinced I was ready to make such a commitment.*

I was unwilling to make such a false statement. I knew I loved her—as a sister. But I wasn't sure I loved her as I would be required (by God) to love her if she was my wife. I wasn't sure I was ready to make that kind of commitment to her. And so I refused to tell her, "I love you," in that special way. It wouldn't have been true. Or, perhaps more accurately—especially toward the end of our pre-engagement relationship—I couldn't be *sure* that it was true. And so, being unsure of its validity, I refused to tell her I loved her.

As soon as I was sure, then I told her: not only that I loved her but that I wanted to commit myself to her to be her husband.

11

HOW DO BROTHERS AND SISTERS GET MARRIED?

QUESTION: It seems to me you think people should go straight from being "just friends" to being engaged. Is that true? Isn't there room for some kind of intermediate step?

ANSWER: You've perceived correctly. I do believe people should go straight from being friends to being engaged. What other kind of relationship with full "Yes, yes" or "No, no" commitments is there?

QUESTION: I don't know. But what you're proposing seems too weird.

ANSWER: I understand your discomfort, but, sorry, the only kind of in-betweenness I know of is when one person in the relationship is ready to make a marriage commitment and the other is not—or isn't *sure* about making a commitment. For instance, I could have proposed to Sarita and she could have said, "I'm not sure." That would have been an in-between state.

But even in such an in-between situation, our communication would have to be simple and straightforward: "I want to commit myself to you. I am willing to commit myself to you. Are you willing to commit yourself to me?" Not, "I'm really thinking of making a commitment to you," or, "I think I'm about ready to be committed to you." What does that mean? *Are* you committed or not? Are you *ready* to be committed or not?"

Brothers and sisters don't give halfway commitments. For brothers and sisters it's either all or nothing. Scripture doesn't allow in-between commitments. Either you're "Yes, yes" or "No, no." Not "Yes, maybe, I hope."

🐦 🐦 🐦

QUESTION: On a slightly different vein: Isn't it asking a bit much to expect a couple to go from no physical-sexual intimacy to "all the way" in one night?

ANSWER: Not necessarily. There are societies in our world that do not allow any physical-sexual intimacy between a husband and wife before they're married. In these societies a bride and groom may never even *meet* until their wedding day. I don't have statistics on the sexual problems such husbands and wives experience, but I don't imagine they are in any worse shape than most American couples.

But be that as it may, I would say that low-level physical-sexual intimacy—the kind of intimacy that most Christian leaders currently accept within boyfriend-girlfriend relationships: hugging, kissing, hand-holding—is quite all right before the wedding night *within the bounds of engagement*.

Sarita and I hugged and kissed and held hands during our engagement. At the same time, let me tell you, there were occasions when we would be walking along and I would let go of her hand. "I'm sorry," I would say. "I can't take it!" And she would look at me: "What's the matter with you?" I didn't go into graphic detail in response to her questions, but the fact was, I was being "turned on," and I knew it would be better for my thought-life and personal sense of self-control if we refrained from holding hands for the time being than if we continued walking down the lane as if nothing were happening inside my mind and body. Sex, as Jesus makes clear in Matthew 5:27 and 28, is not merely a physical reality. It is mental. My "right hand" may not be doing sin, but it may be causing my mind to sin, and so I have to maintain careful control of both my physical actions and my thought life.

One night we were sitting reading *Winnie the Pooh*. I had my arm around Sarita's waist. After about half an hour, she closed the book, turned to me, and wanted to be kissed. I kissed her about one nibble's worth and said, "I'm sorry, but I'm afraid we're going to have to stop!"

"'Stop'?!" she cried. "We haven't even started!"

"Maybe you haven't," I replied miserably, "but I'm already too far."

On our wedding night and in the days that followed, Sarita came to understand a bit better how a male (this male, anyway) responds to sexual stimuli!

ᵃ ᵃ ᵃ

QUESTION: Why do you make such a big deal of waiting until you're *engaged* before getting involved in physical-sexual intimacy?

ANSWER: You don't want to be involved in physical-sexual intimacy before you're engaged because before engagement it can only serve to confuse you and your brother about what kind of commitments you have.

Put in a more positive way, once you're engaged, you're already committed to marrying each other. In that context, physical-sexual intimacy can serve as a confirmation of the commitments you've already made to one another.

ᵃ ᵃ ᵃ

QUESTION: I've always thought of engagement as a time of testing to see if you're really meant for each other; so what kind of commitment are you talking about when you say two people are committed to each other in engagement?

ANSWER: I guess you can take the word *engagement* and apply any definition you want to it. If you want, then, you can say engagement is a time of testing. But what do you mean by that?

What would you be trying to test out during your engagement? Your love? Your faithfulness? Your compatibility?

If you're good enough friends—the kind of friends you should be before you become engaged—you should know each other well enough not to have to question whether you're compatible, loyal, compassionate, the kind of people who can live together peacefully, joyfully, and with glory being given to God.

Engagement isn't just a time for you and your future wife to get to know each other. The purpose of engagement, as I see it, is to make final preparations for marriage: specifically, for the wedding. If it's also a time of testing, then I would have to say that the words with which you and your partner engage yourselves have no more value than the vows with which boyfriends and girlfriends and "serious" daters get themselves entangled, and engagement, then, is nothing more than a slightly formalized version of a boyfriend-girlfriend relationship.

According to social custom, boyfriend-girlfriend and "serious" dating vows can be broken at a moment's notice: "I am committed to being your boyfriend as long as I remain committed," or, "I want you to hold yourself on reserve for marriage for as long as I continue to feel the way I do toward you right now . . . and as long as nothing else comes in the way."

When you become engaged, one person, the man usually, says something to the effect that, "I want to marry you. I don't merely have a feeling like I want to marry you, but I'm *committed* to marrying you—if you're willing to be committed to marrying me." And the other person responds with words to the effect that, "Yes. I'd like to marry you, too. I am willing to be your wife (or husband)." And so they commit themselves to marry each other.

Now what are you suggesting? That a couple shouldn't say such things? That they should merely say in words what boyfriends and girlfriends say in action? That they should say, "I'm feeling a little bit stronger about my resolve to marry you, so I want to put in a definite reservation for us getting married—definite, that is, unless I find I'm not so sure"?

Come on! When will the "real" vows come? At the wedding? You've been unwilling to make unrestricted, "Yes, yes" kinds of vows or promises before. What's to keep your marriage vows from being similarly tentative: "Julie, I do thee hereby wed, for better or worse, richer or poorer, in sickness and in health—unless I realize this was a mistake"?

If you've read chapter 4, you're familiar with the Scriptures that talk about making vows and not meaning them. I believe God is serious when He says our "Yes" must mean "Yes", and our "No," "No." *Don't become engaged until and unless you're willing to stick with it.*

QUESTION: All right. I guess my problem isn't knowing whether I'll remain faithful to my commitments. But how can I know if my future wife is the kind of person who will stick to her commitment?

ANSWER: Again, that's what friendship is for. You know which ones of your friends are faithful, don't you? I know which ones of my friends I trust and to what extent I trust them! My best friends I trust implicitly. (I don't have too many best friends!)

In our society, anyway, in which personal commitment rather than social pressure holds a marriage together, your husband or wife had better be your best friend. And he or she had better be your best friend *before* you get married or engaged.

QUESTION: Is friendship or a "brother-sister relationship" enough? I mean, can a brother-sister relationship adequately test another person's resolve to stick to a commitment?

ANSWER: Let me ask you: is *engagement* enough?

If you're expecting engagement—or a boyfriend-girlfriend or so-called "serious" relationship, for that matter—to provide an adequate test for the kind of loyalty, faithfulness, or devotion required to hold a marriage together for thirty years—forget it! The only thing that will fully test those characteristics is marriage. And, be assured, you and your spouse will receive a full and adequate test in this regard once you're married!

What I'm saying is, engagement won't provide you any more information than a boyfriend-girlfriend relationship will. And a boyfriend-girlfriend relationship won't help you any more than a brother-sister relationship will. So why settle for less than the best? Go with the honesty and integrity of brother-sister relationships. Forget the sham of boyfriend-girlfriend relationships or engagement as a time of testing.

Acquire all the information you can about this potential future spouse while you're still brother and sister. Watch how she interacts with parents, friends, and brothers and sisters in the flesh. You'll get to know whether you can trust her.

ᶻᵃ ᶻᵃ ᶻᵃ

QUESTION: How can you know if you should marry somebody?

ANSWER: There are two major questions I asked myself and that I think you should ask yourself before you get married.

First: *Are you and the person you're thinking of marrying friends? Are you good friends? Best friends? The best friends either of you have ever had?*

Do you enjoy being together and doing the same kinds of things? Do you know each other thoroughly? Do you trust each other implicitly because you know each other? Do you have a strong affection for one another?

If your answer is yes to all of these questions or the one big question, then you and your friend are good potential candidates for marriage.

Think of the marriage relationships with which you're familiar. Think of relationships you know that are dying or that have already broken up. Personally, I don't know of any relationships that have broken up because the husband or wife was unskilled in the area of physical-sexual intimacy. I don't know of any relationships that have broken up because they weren't strong enough in their demands for ownership or exclusiveness. In every case with which I'm familiar, the reason a marriage has broken up is because the husband or wife (or both of them) failed to know, love, and trust the other. They were often very good at demanding their rights; the place where they failed was in giving their love. They were so concerned about themselves and their own interests that they didn't spend the time or make the effort to know, understand, and love the other:

The husband sat watching TV while the wife read a book. The wife put all her efforts into serving the kids while the husband put his efforts into his job. The wife went out to play bridge while the husband went out with "the boys." The husband spent money on his hobby while the wife spent money on hers. The husband demanded his way and the wife demanded hers. They spent little if any time together. They rarely talked. They had fewer and fewer interests in common. They had more and more interests apart. They lost their affection for one another. One or the other of them decided their marriage was "dead" and filed for divorce.

In fact, what had died—if it had ever been alive to begin with—was not their marriage. It was their friendship. A good, fulfilling marriage is based not only on the wedding vows, but on true knowledge, affection, and trust: friendship.

Yet with all that I have just said about friendship, there is something else that is still more important. You and your spouse may be great friends, but if your lives don't have a common purpose, you're in for trouble!

So, second: *Are you and the person you're thinking of marrying pursuing the same goals and objectives?* As separate individuals, are you pursuing the same goals you would want to pursue together as a couple?

God made Adam in order to do a job: to "rule over the fish of the sea and the birds of the air, over the livestock, over all the earth, and over all the creatures that move along the ground" (Genesis 1:26; see also Genesis 1:28; 2:15). Eve was made and given to Adam to help Adam do his job (Genesis 2:18, 20b). God has given you a job to do. And if He intends for you to marry, one of His chief reasons is because He knows you can do a better job with your husband helping you than if you tried to do it on your own.

The Apostle Paul talks about this in 2 Corinthians 6:14. He warns us not to let ourselves be "unequally yoked."

A yoke hooks two animals together so they're forced to walk side by side. The reason you yoke animals together is so they can work toward a common goal. If two animals pull together, they can either do harder things—things that neither one of them could do alone, or they can work longer without a rest: neither of them will have to work as hard, so neither of them will get tired as quickly. That's the idea behind a yoke.

A yoke is helpful, however, only when the animals are fairly well matched. If one of them is much larger than the other, or if one is a willing worker while the other is obstinate, there's going to be trouble! In that case, if any work is to be done, one animal will do it all. The other will be dragged along for the ride or will try to go anywhere but the direction he should be going. Any way you look at it, an unequal yoking is a sad state of affairs!

Marriage is a yoking—a tying together of two people to accomplish a task. If you're to have a helper or to be a helper, you need to be yoked with someone who, before God, is willingly trying to do a task similar to your own. In 2 Corinthians 6:14, Paul told us not to be unequally yoked with *unbelievers*. If you are a follower of Jesus Christ, you will always be unequally yoked if you try hitching yourself to someone who follows another god. I don't care what name that god has—it might be the name of the person you want to marry: if you are committed to following Jesus and your partner is following someone else, you're in trouble. Until one of you decides to follow the beat of the "other drummer," both of you will be in a constant tug-of-war. "We need to go this way!" "No! We need to go that!"

"No one can serve two masters," said Jesus. "Either he will hate the one and love the other, or he will be devoted to the one and despise the other" (Matthew 6:24). You have to choose whom you will follow.

But while it is always foolish for a Christian to marry a non-Christian, it can be equally foolish for two followers of Christ, even committed Christians, to marry. Two Christians can be as poorly yoked as a Christian and a non-Christian. The reason is simple: Jesus doesn't want us all to do the same kind of work. As we read in 1 Corinthians 12, there are many parts to the body of

Christ, and each one has its own job to do. The question you must answer is, "What task has God called me to fulfill?"

You and your brother are both supposed to bless the world—but how? Has God called you to plant churches among Muslims? You may have a tough time being yoked to someone whose life dream is to make $100,000 a year. If your goal is to raise a family and perhaps minister to unwed mothers, I would say it would probably be unwise for you to marry someone whose job will take him away from home twenty weeks of the year.

So, to what has God called you? And to what has He called the brother whom you're thinking of marrying? Will you be equally yoked if you marry? Are you pursuing the same goals?

If you and the one you're thinking of marrying are friends together; if you are not only friends, but the very best friends either of you have ever had; if both of you are committed to the same goals and objectives; if you are committed not only to the same general goals and objectives, but very specific goals and objectives; if you're running in the same direction and seem fairly well matched; then you can begin seriously considering whether or not you ought to marry.

Sarita and I became friends. Then good friends. Best friends. Very best friends. The very best friends either of us had ever had. We were comfortable in one another's presence. We could talk about everything. We *did* talk about everything. And while we talked and while we grew in our knowledge, affection, and trust, we discovered our lives meshed. We were running the same race. We had the same goals. We encouraged each other. We made a great team.

And so, eventually, we committed ourselves to become a husband-and-wife team. That was the day we got engaged.

And then we were married.

ੴ ੴ ੴ

QUESTION: Taking this a step further: would you please comment on when two people should become engaged?

ANSWER: Positively speaking, you should become engaged when you are ready to get married. More negatively, you're not ready to become engaged if you don't meet the criteria for getting married (see the question above). Don't let your desire to enjoy the privileges of marriage push you to become engaged prematurely.

I recommend two criteria to help you tell if you're ready to be engaged.

First, if before you heard about the idea of treating your brothers and sisters as brothers and sisters you would be only boyfriend and girlfriend with this person you're thinking of marrying, then you're not ready to be engaged.

Take note! The reason people want to be boyfriend-girlfriend is because, though they desire to enjoy the privileges of marriage—"to have and to hold" each other—they don't want to commit themselves to marriage's responsibilities. They know they can't make such a commitment: not now, not honestly.

Boyfriends and girlfriends are people who may want to make a "forever" commitment *one day*, but realize right now that something stands in their way. Perhaps they're too young or they don't have enough money. Maybe they're afraid of their parents' anger if they should get married. Most likely, they don't know or trust each other well enough to commit themselves "for better or worse . . . till death do us part." And so they become boyfriend-girlfriend: committed "like married" but not really.

Take note of what your conscience is saying in this matter. Maybe you're not prepared to make the kinds of commitments one makes in a marriage relationship. Maybe you're too young. Maybe you could make the commitments, but your relationship hasn't progressed to the point where you feel confident about entering marriage with this other person.

Don't get engaged simply because that is a more "honest" form of boyfriend-girlfriend relationship than a boyfriend-girlfriend relationship itself. *If you're not ready to be engaged, then don't get engaged.*

Second, you're not ready for engagement if you haven't received counsel from both sets of parents and haven't received their permission and blessing for being married.

I use those words—*counsel, permission,* and *blessing*—carefully. You need all three. You need much more than your parents' mere acquiescence to a decision and commitment you've already made. You need their *permission* because they are responsible before God to care for you. (See chapter 6 about who owns you.) You need their *blessing* and *counsel* because they can and will either help your relationship or hinder it.

QUESTION: If I were to ask my parents for their permission, all they'd say is, "You have to make your own decisions; it's your life!"

ANSWER: They may be saying one of two things by that—and you'd better find out which one! One is good, the other is not so good.

Either they are saying, "Johnny, we became convinced long ago that you are mature enough to make your own decisions. At that time we gave you permission to do whatever you believed you should do. If you believe this is the right decision, then of course you have our permission!" Or they are saying, "Johnny, we don't believe you really want our input. We're convinced you've already made up your mind. What you really want us to do is rubber stamp a decision you've already made. We can't and won't do that. We have some real reservations about your relationship. At the same time, however, since you obviously want to marry Paula, we won't stand in your way."

If this latter statement more nearly reflects what your parents are saying, you have a problem that needs to be dealt with. Your parents have probably tried to give you advice and direction in the past, and you have proven unwilling to listen or obey. If this is the case, then you need to confess your foolishness and ask your parents' forgiveness. And then you need to strenuously pursue them until you get the input and commitment you require.

Receive their input. Ask such questions as, "If Paula and I were to pursue marriage, what would you be concerned about in terms of our personal strengths and weaknesses?" "What hurdles do you see us needing to overcome before we make wedding plans?"

Get their commitment. Ask questions like these: "Are you able and willing to bless us in this relationship?" "Will you support us in this relationship? We're not planning such a thing, but suppose one or the other of us decided to quit the relationship: would you do everything you could to help us work through our problems and to stay together?"

Of course if you ask questions like these, you may expect some fairly pointed questions in return! For instance: "What plans do you have in terms of housing, jobs, kids . . . ?" "How confident are you of your relationship?"

When the dust settles from all this question-and-answering, I am convinced you will find this course of action will improve your relationship with both sets of parents. It is a sign of maturity when a person sincerely seeks advice, counsel, and direction. Most parents and in-laws are pleased when their children are mature and marry mature people! Further, since your parents do have caretaking responsibilities toward you, it should set their minds and hearts at ease that you want them to know what you are doing and that you want their input about it.

Depending on how well you listen to and follow their advice, you will be establishing with your parents and in-laws a base for open communication in the future. More than that, by discussing these things with your parents, you and your future spouse will be strengthening your commitment to fulfill your responsibilities one to another. It will help you assure yourselves that you are truly becoming *engaged* and not merely faking yourselves out with boyfriend-girlfriend infatuation.

QUESTION: What if a person has been out of the house and on his own for several years? For instance, I haven't lived in my parents' home for over ten years. Do you really think they can give me good advice about whom I should marry?

ANSWER: Absolutely! And you should seek it.

QUESTION: What if my parents are messed up in their own lives? For instance, my parents have now both been divorced twice and want nothing to do with Christ. Beyond that, my dad's an alcoholic.

ANSWER: Even in your case, I believe God wants you to get your parents' counsel, permission, and blessing. Their counsel must be weighed against Scripture, of course, and you may have serious doubts about the value of their blessing; they may be so far gone that they can do little if anything to be of service to you and your spouse. But neither of these things is an excuse to ignore their counsel, their blessing, or their permission.

QUESTION: My parents are dead. What should I do?

ANSWER: I would seek counsel from some other people whom I respect and know to be wise and godly. I would ask similar questions of them that I would ask of my parents.

QUESTION: What if my parents won't give their blessing?

ANSWER: If either set of parents will not give you their blessing and support, you'd better go back and get their input: "Why won't you bless us? What stands in the way of such a blessing? Is there anything—and if so, what is it—we can do to overcome these hurdles?"

There *is* wisdom in many counselors (see Proverbs 15:22), and it is certainly better to receive a blessing than to live under a curse, whether spoken or not. You are not your own. Make sure all interested parties (that means everyone who has a legitimate share in determining your future, everyone who has a caregiving responsibility toward you—including your parents) are given adequate opportunities to direct your course.

ta ta ta

QUESTION: How do I pursue marriage and still remain "brother-sister" or "just friends?" I don't understand. If I begin pursuing marriage, won't I be breaking one of the rules of brother-sister relationships? I mean, I wouldn't be treating my sister as a sister! Also, I have a bunch of questions I need to ask this girl before I would be ready to ask her to marry me—questions like how many children she would want, what her attitudes are toward birth control and disciplining kids, . . . things like that. If I ask her these kinds of questions, though, I wouldn't be treating her like a sister anymore. How would you deal with this kind of situation?

ANSWER: Good questions!

You pursue marriage and remain brother-sister by being aggressively honest with your sister (and your other brothers and sisters) about what your desires and interests are. You admit that you have a strong desire to get married. You tell your brothers and sisters that marriage is a concern of yours. You're up-front with them about what's on your mind.

I don't think you need to raise your sister's expectations by saying, "I'm wondering if I should marry *you*." She doesn't need to know—and it really isn't her business to know—where she stands on your list of potential mates. But you can, and, I believe in your circumstances it would be a *good idea* for you to tell your brothers and sisters that you're concerned about getting married.

QUESTION: Wait. You're saying do this with men *and* women?

ANSWER: Yes. Not everyone you meet, but a few close friends, brothers and sisters whom you trust.

Is it on your heart? Is it a concern to you? Then share it with them. Pray about it with them. That's part of what friendship and brother-sister relationships are all about.

QUESTION: Two questions. First, *why* share it? And, second, if I do talk about it with women, won't I be opening myself up to the problems you had when you talked with Sally about your desires toward Carrie? Wouldn't I be putting myself in the position of raising somebody's hopes or expectations?

ANSWER: Again, excellent questions.

First, as far as why share your concerns and desires: because it will let your friends know what's on your heart and where you're coming from. It will help them understand you, pray for you, and maybe even help you. Your friends—guys and girls, men and women—may know some wonderful woman whom you don't know. Maybe they can introduce you. There are all kinds of reasons why you would want to share these things with trusted friends.

But then as far as leading on your sisters: the way you avoid that is by being very up-front about what you're doing and what you're meaning. Again, you don't tell a sister, "I'm interested in marrying *you*." You're not proposing marriage; you're not suggesting or pleading for marriage; you're making no commitments and implying no commitments. What you're doing is sharing these things with her because you value her friendship, her insights, her judgment, her prayers. You're doing with her what you would do, and *are* doing, with other close friends.

Make it clear that *even if you have feelings for her* (and quite possibly you do—and that's okay, and you may even tell her that you have feelings), *you're unwilling that those feelings should be the basis for a commitment.* You're looking for more than feelings—yours or hers—to lead you to marriage. You're looking for character, integrity, values, goals, aspirations. You're looking for a woman with whom you can be equally yoked. Maybe she's the one, maybe she's not. But the reason you're sharing these things with her is because she's your friend, she's your sister, she's someone you trust. You're *not* sharing it with her because she's potential marriage material.

QUESTION: But wait! That *is* the reason I'm sharing it.

ANSWER: I hope not! She may *be* potential marriage material, but that fact ought not to be what provides the motive for your sharing your heart with her. The reason you should be telling this sister—the reason you should be telling *anyone* about what's on your heart—is because she or he can help you: provide you leads, give you insights, critique your line of reasoning, pray for you.

If you are carefully, diligently, consistently honest in the way you express yourself to your brothers and sisters, you're not going to raise any girl's expectations. You may raise a few eyebrows—"Wow! Here's a guy who really knows what he wants!"—but you're not going to raise expectations.

QUESTION: Okay. Now what about that matter of asking questions?
ANSWER: Right.
Before I answer your question, let me just say here: you're on the right track when you put the matter of asking questions together with the idea of pursuing marriage. One of the best ways to pursue marriage is by asking this sister of yours lots of questions and listening carefully to her replies.
But in response to your question: just *ask the questions*. Ask them directly. Ask them in the way a friend would ask another: because you value your sister's opinions, because you know you can gain valuable insights by discussing these issues with her, because you would gain valuable insights by discussing these issues with *anyone*.

QUESTION: But I wouldn't talk about birth control and how many kids they would want with just anyone!
ANSWER: Maybe you should! Not *anyone*, but friends whose opinions you trust, people whose thinking has stimulated you in the past.
Don't you think it would be valuable to talk with your sister about these things even if you weren't considering marrying her?

QUESTION: Well, yeah, but . . . !
ANSWER: You ought to be interested enough in what your sister thinks that no matter what she says—even if you decide she isn't the woman for you—you'll be glad you talked to her. She stimulated your thinking; she got you to think thoughts you never thought before. Or, if she didn't stimulate your thinking, you stimulated hers.

If you value your sister, if you value her opinions and she values yours, it shouldn't matter whether you're in the last stages of considering marriage or not. If these issues are important to you, you should want to know what your sister thinks and you should want her to know what you think: because it's good for you to know each other.

Again, you should want to know not only because you want to find out what she thinks, but because you want to grow as a result of your interaction. You want *you* to grow and you want *her* to grow.

Perhaps you'll want to ask some of your questions in a group context where a bunch of people will be able to be blessed all at one time. A discussion like the one you're suggesting could be *most* stimulating and valuable to everyone who participates.

But let me back off for a minute. Let me tell you what my deepest concern is here.

You're saying you want to get to know your sister. You want her open, honest, no-holds-barred opinion. Certainly you would rather have that than some dressed-up varnish job. Well suppose you tell her, "I'm thinking of marrying you and the following twenty questions will help me make my decision." Then you start asking the questions. What is she supposed to say? Suddenly she's confronted with too many variables. Now it's not merely the questions she must answer—how many children she wants, what she believes about discipline, whether she believes in birth control or not—but she has to decide whether or not she wants to marry you. *And that second decision mucks up her thinking process.*

Suppose she *doesn't* want to marry you? Or suppose she doesn't *know* if she wants to marry you? A woman in that situation is going to have a far more urgent sense that she needs to clarify her attitude toward marrying you than that she needs to answer a question about children. If you are truly interested in discovering her opinion—which, I'm saying, you should be, even if you're not going to marry each other—you will have destroyed your chances before you began.

And if she *does* want to marry you? Suddenly she will realize that her entire future could rest on her answer to a single question. How she responds could spell the difference between her being your Mrs. Right or being Nobody. How should she answer? Should she curb her honest opinion for the sake of avoiding offense? What if she overstates or misstates her feelings in the matter? Can she be totally honest with you?

Give her a break! Let her be herself. Let you be yourself. Talk to each other openly without the issue of marriage coming in between. The time will arrive soon enough for you both to know whether you're meant for one another.

QUESTION: Could you give some examples of how you might ask personal questions?

ANSWER: Okay. You want to know what your sister thinks about kids. Ask, "Have you ever thought of how many kids you'd want if you were to marry?" Or make a statement: "I was just reading this article where they urge people to have no more than two kids. I think that's a ridiculous idea!"

You want to know how your sister thinks about becoming a missionary. Ask, "Have you ever thought of being a missionary?" or state: "Y'know, I've wanted to be a missionary all my life!"

You want to know how she believes children ought to be disciplined. Start a conversation by asking, "When you were growing up, how did your parents discipline you?" or say, "I was thinking about the way my parents brought me up. Sometimes it makes me angry. I think if I ever have kids, I'm going to do things differently."

I've found that friends, brothers and sisters who know each other well, can ask or say almost anything in one another's presence and in almost any context—in the middle of a group or privately. They don't imply to one another anything about commitments they can't or don't intend to make.

QUESTION: It seems to me that if a person were to ask a lot of questions the way you've suggested, the person who's answering will soon catch on to what the questioner is thinking about. If someone were to ask me a lot of questions related to after-marriage kinds of things, I'd know what they were getting at.

ANSWER: So this sister "catches on" and decides to ask, "Why are you asking me all of these questions?" And you want to say, "Because I'm thinking of marrying you."

Well, fine. That's true. But it's only part of the truth. If you have the right attitude, it should be only one among many motivating factors. You should also be able to say with equal honesty, "Because I'm thinking of marriage in general." "Because I value your opinion." "Because I'm curious." "Because I find whenever I talk to you, you make me think in ways I've never thought before." "Because I'd like to put my ideas to the test and you seem like a good tester." "Because I know you'll tell me honestly what you think and other people aren't always so honest."

So you want to tell her you're thinking of marrying her? Tell her! Only tell her all these other things as well so she gets the right idea.

In fact, let me put it to you this way: if you *can't* honestly tell her all these other things, then you can't be very serious about marrying her. It would certainly be foolish to think you're serious about marrying her. If you can't say all these other things, you don't value her enough to be thinking of marrying her.

Yes. Marriage is an issue. But it's only one among many issues. And both you and your sister know that you have valid reasons for asking questions like the ones you've suggested, whether she's interested in marrying you or not.

So engage your sister in conversation: "I think, if I were married and was able to have a family, I'd want a *dozen* kids."

"Oh! That's a *crazy* idea! . . ."

You'll have an open, honest, free-wheeling discussion—the kind of discussion friends have.

ॐ ॐ ॐ

QUESTION: Your advice sounds positively dangerous to me! You're opening people up to all kinds of abuse. In my experience, when a guy and girl merely spend *time* together, they tend to raise each other's expectations. And now you're telling them not only to spend time together, but to talk about their concerns over whether or not they'll get married. I think that's insane.

ANSWER: Sarita and I talked about marriage. We talked about our goals and aspirations. We talked about what we would want in a marriage partner, what our beliefs were about raising a family, how many kids we thought we might want. We talked about all these things and we raised no expectations.

You avoid raising expectations by being rigorously consistent in your treatment of one another as brother and sister. If you refuse to imply you are making a commitment until the moment you are ready to *make* the commitment; if you do everything you can to consistently and clearly communicate the message, "I am not interested in making a commitment to you. I am unable to make a commitment to you. I simply want to be your friend; therefore I will treat you as a friend," you will raise no expectations. No one will be confused. The point is *consistency*—consistency at all times and in every way. If and when you do fail to treat each other as brother and sister, then you need to repent of your failure and ask forgiveness, but at all times and in every way, you must seek to communicate: "I'm your brother. You're my sister. I'm not your boyfriend. You're not my girlfriend. I'm not committed to you and you have no business being committed to me—no more than we're committed to any other brothers or sisters."

Brother-sister relationships are possible even on the way to marriage. Brothers and sisters talk about everything openly, honestly, and consistently. Boyfriends, girlfriends, and "serious" daters talk about everything too, except not really. They play games. They toy with each other's emotions. They hint at marriage. They imply, insinuate, and infer. They flirt and play around with romance and physical-sexual intimacy. They talk about feelings and desires, interests and dreams, but they *never talk about commitment*. That's where the problems come in. They're not totally honest with one another.

I'm saying, drop the guile. Be consistent. Be honest. Make commitment—open, honest, *explicit* commitment—an issue in your relationships. Make it a big issue. It *is* a big issue whether you want it to be or not. So give it its rightful place.

12

JUST A FEW MORE QUESTIONS!

QUESTION: I have a major problem with your brother-sister idea. It has to do with the matter of feelings. I think I'd die of asphyxiation if I had to hide my feelings the way you seem to think a person should! You're so into your brain. Where does the *heart* come in? Where does *romance* come in?

ANSWER: I appreciate your question and sympathize with what you're trying to say. I agree: romance and heart and feelings can be fun. But they can also be devastating. So before you challenge my "cold, heartless, and unemotional" approach, please be sure you know to what you're objecting.

My convictions are not based on an aversion to emotions. I have emotions and I enjoy them. Sarita calls me an "old softie" because I'll break down and cry over silly stories or touching scenes in a movie. And as far as romance goes, I know the thrill of first-blush love. I know the giddy excitement of holding "her" gaze a moment longer than social conventions normally allow. I've experienced the weak-kneed pleasure of holding "her" hand and saying, "I love you."

I've also experienced the enervating heartache of having someone who said she loved me tell me she wants to break up. And I've observed the desperate grief of other people who have been abandoned. I've known men and women who have wept bitter tears, threatened or attempted suicide, been paralyzed with grief for weeks and months. Why? All because their "one and only true love" has suddenly become untrue.

So, yes. Enjoy the thrill of romance, the warmth of being loved, the pleasure of a heart that's full. But take an honest look at both sides of the picture. For every thrill you offer to encourage me to talk unreservedly about my good feelings toward a member of the opposite sex, I will offer you another of emotional devastation.

But look, stories, positive or negative, are insufficient grounds for judging our actions. If there were no pleasure in telling a woman you loved her, if there were no joy in having a sexual encounter, if there were no potential for pain in these things, we would still have to answer to the Lord about His commands. And so I'm convinced there is more upon which to base our decisions than mere pleasure or pain. I've outlined some of these principles elsewhere, especially in chapters 4 and 5.

Before moving on, however, I would like to comment a bit more about the idea of romance.

I think most people think of romance in terms of candlelit dinners, flowers, walks in the moonlight, stars in your eyes, and "happily ever after." If their definition is correct, I wish them good luck in finding romance. I don't know anyone who has lived a life of unmitigated romance by that definition. Sarita and I have a great relationship, but even for us there have been times when the stars in our eyes were like the stars you see on cartoons after one of the characters has been bashed over the head!

I think most of us should look for romance of a different kind—a romance that can work in real life and on an ongoing basis. I'm not saying you should give up on ever enjoying fancy dinners, flowers, walks in the moonlight, etc. But I think you should put your efforts elsewhere.

What are you looking for in marriage? I hope it's not starry-eyed wonder and excitement. What most people are looking for, I believe, is intimacy—intimacy that shows itself in knowledge, affection, and trust: "I know you as you really are; you know me as

I am; we like each other anyway and trust each other to stick together." To me, that's romance. Over the long haul, that's what brings the pleasure in marriage.

When Sarita is pregnant, she becomes deathly ill. With Amy, our firstborn, she lost thirty-six pounds before she gained an ounce. For a while, she couldn't even drink a glass of water without throwing up.

During those months of terrible ill health, I went to work during the day while Sarita laid in bed. As I remember it, I called her at home occasionally just to find out how she was doing. In the evenings, I came home, made myself some dinner, tried to find something she could eat without throwing up, and then sat by the bed and talked with her. We didn't have candles. We didn't have wild, passionate sex. We had quiet hours of fellowship.

I think of the two types of flame a blowtorch produces—one when it is first lit, and the other after it has been tuned. At the moment a blowtorch is lit it makes a loud *Pop*—almost a bang—and the flame billows up. It's quite exciting to watch! But for all the wonder and excitement that flame produces, it isn't useful! You can burn yourself on it. You can heat something with it. But you can't cut a piece of metal or weld something together. Only when the flame is tuned to a sharp, controlled point will it accomplish the task a blowtorch is especially designed to do. It's the same way with romance. Romance is great when it's disciplined by the demands of God's righteousness.

I know plenty of couples who have entered marriage with flames of "romance" popping and soaring hundreds of feet in the air. Today they have no romance at all. They don't have a bonfire of romance; they don't have a campfire; they don't have a flickering flame; they don't even have smoldering coals. Instead, they've "enjoyed" towering infernos of romance that burned up their marriages and, in some cases, their souls. Many of these friends of mine are still picking through the ashes of "what should have been." They're either divorced or on their way in that direction. Why? Because they didn't discipline themselves by God's standards.

ea ea ea

QUESTION: I'd like to keep on this topic of romance a moment. At the end of chapter 7 there's a question where readers are asked to define and differentiate between several terms: friendly affection, romantic interest or attraction, sexual interest or attraction, sexual activity, sexual involvement, sexual intercourse, physical-sexual intimacy, etc. Would you please define and differentiate those terms for us?

ANSWER: *Friendly affection* is the kind of desire two friends have for one another; there are no sexual overtones. Friendly affection can be mild or extremely powerful; it can range from what we might call fondness all the way up to love. In its more powerful forms, friendly affection can lead a person to make all manner of sacrifices for the benefit of the friend.

Romantic interest or attraction is friendly affection with sexual overtones. It is interest in a person that includes the sexual side: the promise or possibility of marital-style privileges and commitments.

Sexual interest or attraction is what is added to friendly affection to come up with romantic interest or attraction. It's interest in a person that arises because of that person's sexual nature, his or her gender identity.

Sexual activity is any kind of behavior that is sexually stimulating or arises from the sexual side of our nature.

Sexual involvement is sexual activity *with another person*. It is the same thing as *sexual intercourse* in the broad sense of that term: sexual dealings between two people.

Sexual intercourse, of course, has two uses: one in the narrow sense that it is generally used within our culture—"going all the way," having a man penetrate a woman's vagina with his penis; the other is the broad sense we mentioned above: sexual dealings between two people, with *or without* physical contact.

Physical-sexual intimacy is sexual intercourse, broadly speaking, with a physical component. In other words, it includes physical contact. As I suggested in chapter 7, a couple may be involved in sexual intercourse without touching each other physically. If it weren't for our culture's narrow use of the term *sexual intercourse* (and of the word *intercourse* itself), I would have just as soon spoken of physical-sexual intercourse as of physical-sexual intimacy. We would have then also spoken of physical-social intercourse and physical-emotional intercourse. As it is, I coined a new term: physical-sexual intimacy.

Coitus refers to the act that in our culture has become commonly referred to as sexual intercourse: the penetration of a woman's vagina by a man's penis. I guess if we were to become extremely technical about it, coitus is not complete until there has been an ejaculation, hence the term *coitus interruptus*, referring to withdrawal of the penis before ejaculation.

Physical-emotional intimacy and *physical-social intimacy* I defined rather carefully in chapter 7: they refer to physical contact that communicates emotional or social messages.

The upshot of all these terms is this: brothers and sisters engage in physical-emotional and physical-social intimacy. They also have and are willing to express friendly affection for one another. If they are sexually or romantically attracted to or interested in another person (which they might be), they refuse to express this attraction or interest in action, and, if they ever decide that they must express it in words, they make sure they express it carefully (see chapter 5).

Brothers and sisters refuse to become sexually involved or to participate in sexual intercourse, physical-sexual intimacy, or coitus prior to or outside of marriage.

ﻩ ﻩ ﻩ

QUESTION: I have a complaint about your view of sexual activity. You make it sound as if holding hands or kissing before marriage is as bad as "going all the way." As far as you're concerned, they're all the same thing: they communicate the same thing and they're all based on the same false vows or promises.

What bothers me about that view is that instead of discouraging people from the problem of premarital sex—something that's clearly prohibited in Scripture—you talk about things that the

Bible never mentions and you make them all sound like sins. I have a hard time with that.

ANSWER: You're right, the Bible doesn't mention by name the practices of hand-holding, kissing, and so many of the other common practices we are aware of in so-called committed relationships outside of marriage today. But while the Bible doesn't refer to these practices by name, it *does* talk about integrity. And it talks about vows and promises. I think I have adequately demonstrated how hand-holding, kissing, hugging, etc. are intimately related to the slithery, uncommitted "committed" relationships with which we are all familiar. No one I know has ever been able to engage in them with integrity outside of a marriage or engagement commitment.

I think it's interesting that you call premarital sex a "far worse problem" than boyfriend-girlfriend and "serious" relationships, hand-holding, kissing, and all the other practices I've mentioned. In a way, of course, you're right. The social consequences—I mean, the consequences to society as a whole—of people getting AIDS, of unwed mothers, of abortion, etc., are great. They cost a lot of money, not to mention personal heartache, grief, and tragedy.

But as painful as these consequences may be and as costly as they are to society as a whole, I think Christian leaders have failed to accurately assess the costs associated with boyfriends' and girlfriends' lack of integrity in becoming involved in false vows and promises, in obligating themselves to limit their social interaction with other members of the opposite sex, and in all the other practices that are common to our cultural dating patterns but fall outside the limits of brother-sister relationships.

I think the problem is not that I have stressed side issues to the detriment of the central issue. Rather, our society has so downplayed the significance of these factors, that they appear like molehills though they are truly mountains.

I'm merely trying to make people wake up to reality. I'm saying, "Listen. If you're worried about hitting Premarital Sex Street—and tell me of a Christian leader today who is not!— you're worried about the wrong thing. You have to pass a slew of other warning signs long before you ever hit that road. Take notice of the signs along the way. If you're on Boyfriend-Girlfriend Boulevard, if you've passed Ownership Alley or Exclusive City, if you're lying to your brothers and sisters through your speech or conduct: you're on the wrong road! You took a wrong turn back there somewhere. You need to turn around and go back until you hit Brother-Sister Highway. Brother-Sister is a much better way to go. For one thing, it never hits Premarital Sex Street, but for another, it's a better road. It's well paved with few potholes, a *lot* fewer than Boyfriend-Girlfriend Boulevard! It's a great highway to be on: lots of good scenery, great people to travel with. *In every way* it's a superior route to the one you're on to get you where you want to go. I don't care if you want to get to Marriage City or stay in Single Country for the rest of your life. Brother-Sister Highway is the road you want to be on."

ta ta ta

QUESTION: A friend of mine, Shane, wants me to be his girlfriend. Now that I've heard what you have to say, I think I should avoid getting involved in that kind of committed relationship, but I doubt Shane would understand, and even if he did, I'm sure he'd disagree. What should I do?

ANSWER: The first thing you need to do is pray. Pray for understanding. Pray for your understanding of Shane and his understanding of you. Pray also for strength and discernment. Pray that God will touch Shane's heart and mind. Pray that He might give you special words of wisdom to help Shane understand.

After prayer, however, you need to get busy. Don't assume Shane won't understand. Don't assume he'll disagree. Give him the benefit of the doubt. Let the Holy Spirit work in his heart. If this book has helped you, why not loan him a copy? You might find he thinks it's a great idea. On the other hand, maybe he will disagree. Either way, you may find your own thinking being challenged as you discuss these ideas with another person—especially someone who's interested in the subject and interested in you!

Beyond loaning books and talking things over, make sure you're consistent in your behavior. Don't lead him on and make sure he doesn't catch you in a web of unspoken promises and illegitimate feelings of obligation.

Finally, don't feel compelled to break off communication with him. Rather, proceed with caution in your relationship. I give this last piece of advice with the following idea in mind.

The summer before Sarita and I became engaged, we were writing letters back and forth. At one point, she wrote a letter—I don't remember the contents, but I remember it had a feel to it that concerned me. I shared it with some women whom I admired for spiritual insight and discernment. These women said, "Sarita is obviously looking to you for her security. She is wanting you to provide the satisfaction in her life that only God can provide. We'd recommend that you break off your relationship with her."

I thought about that recommendation for a couple of hours, and then rejected it. I realized that if Sarita really were as weak and self-seeking as my counselors implied, then to break off our relationship would be one of the most *un*loving, *un*friendly things I could do. I would be opening her to the attack of the next "loving" guy who came her way.

There are a lot of guys who would be thrilled to have a girlfriend, I thought. A lot of guys would love to have a girl fall at their feet and worship them. But how many guys would love *Sarita*? Assuming my counselors were correct in their assessment of who Sarita was and how she was acting: how many guys would love Sarita enough to refuse her advances and turn her eyes to the Lord? Not many!

I decided that the most friendly, loving thing for me to do was to remain in relationship with Sarita. And anytime she came to me to fulfill all her dreams and wishes or anytime she tried to make me go beyond the bounds of brother-sister commitment, I would say, "I'm sorry. You cannot get your satisfaction from me. You cannot make me into your god! You need to pursue the real God, what He desires, what He wants."

What Sarita needed was a guy who would care for her, understand her, listen to her, love her, and turn her eyes toward the Lord. She didn't need a guy who rejected her. She didn't need a guy who would be willing to take advantage of any foolish notions of love she might have. She needed a guy who would love her enough to be her friend *without* being her boyfriend.

I thought I was just that kind of person. So I pursued a relationship with Sarita—with caution. You proceed with caution, too.

From what you've told me, I don't think you need to stop your relationship with Shane. Instead, love him enough to guide him in paths of righteousness. Be aware of the pitfalls you may encounter. Be on your guard against premature commitment, but love him enough to remain his friend.

ta ta ta

QUESTION: Do you think you should always stay in a relationship with another person? I have a friend, a guy, who will not leave me alone. He's always trying to touch me and poke me. He puts his arms around me and tries to hold me. Sometimes he gets very aggressive and makes clearly sexual advances. I really like him and I don't want to cut off our relationship, but when I tell him I don't want him to do the things I've described, he won't listen to me. He keeps right on doing them anyway. I want to love him with God's kind of love. What should I do?

ANSWER: When talking about traffic control, yellow cautions often turn to red stop lights. The same thing can happen in human relationships. It sounds to me as if your light has turned red. It's time to put on the brakes and bring the relationship to a halt.

If you're giving this friend of yours clear signals that you don't want anything to do with physical-sexual intimacy; if both verbally and physically you are telling him you don't want him touching you or poking you or putting his arms around you, if you're doing these things and he isn't listening to you or responding to your messages, then it is best to cut off the relationship. Obviously, he doesn't respect you enough to listen to what you have to say or to take note of what you need. He's pursuing you for his own pleasure and gain, not in order to be a blessing to you.

Jesus' love is the type that serves other people and seeks their best. Your friend needs to be awakened to his self-centered ways. Perhaps breaking off your relationship with him is the best way to wake him up. It is certainly the best way for you to stay out of the kind of trouble you're bound to fall into if he won't leave you alone.

ﻩﺎ ﻩﺎ ﻩﺎ

QUESTION: I have never thought about relationships the way you describe them. I think you're probably right, but now what? I have a girlfriend. What should I do?

ANSWER: No matter what the cost, do what's right.

The first thing you need to do is make sure you believe what you say you believe. Are you sure *why* you believe what you do about your behavior and your relationship with your girlfriend? Do you think a boyfriend-girlfriend relationship is wrong? Why? Why do you think a brother-sister relationship is right? What, specifically, about *your* relationship is wrong? Are you sure you're really *guilty*, or am I merely an effective guilt-manipulator? You need to be fully convinced in your own mind concerning what you believe (see Romans 14:5).

You'll probably want to write out your thoughts on this matter.

Seek counsel as you build convictions, but once you're convinced of what you believe, don't be swayed by every wind of teaching that may come along (see Ephesians 4:14). A firm foothold on your convictions is a sign of maturity.

If you are fully convinced that you need to abandon your boyfriend-girlfriend relationship, then be encouraged. Though for a moment all discipline is painful, in the end "it produces a harvest of righteousness and peace for those who have been trained by it" (Hebrews 12:11). If you do what's right, you're going to reap a harvest of righteousness and peace.

So what should you do?

First, acknowledge your sin. Confess it to God and to your sister—and seek reconciliation. In Proverbs 6:1–5, Solomon says,

> My son, if you have put up security for your neighbor, if you have struck hands in pledge for another, if you have been trapped by what you said, ensnared by the words of your mouth, then do this, my son, to free yourself, since you have fallen into your neighbor's hands: *Go and humble yourself; press your plea with your neighbor! Allow no sleep to your eyes, no slumber to your eyelids. Free yourself, like a gazelle from the hand of the hunter, like a bird from the snare of the fowler* (emphasis added).

If you are in a boyfriend-girlfriend relationship right now, *you are ensnared.* If you have become involved in implied, lying covenants of marriage, *you're trapped.* "Go and humble yourself; press your plea . . . [and] free yourself." Tell your sister how you've wronged her and what you want to do about it. Ask if she would be willing to forgive you. "If you are offering your gift at the altar and there remember that your brother [sister] has something against you, leave your gift there in front of the altar. First go and be reconciled to your brother [sister]; then come and offer your gift" (Matthew 5:23–24).

You can never pay back your sister for breaking your unspoken boyfriend-girlfriend vow, but your sister may forgive you your debt. So seek forgiveness, and "go and sin no more."

In your case, "sinning no more" may mean one of two things: either you need to move on toward marriage (make explicit vows, promises, and commitments, and keep them), or both of you need to back off and return to being just friends.

To become friends again, to treat one another as brother and sister, you and your girlfriend may find you need to let your relationship cool off awhile; you may need to leave each other completely alone. Ask the Lord and wise counselors who know you and your girlfriend well for advice about what specific steps you should take in this regard.

‡a ‡a ‡a

I think we've covered the main topics you need to know in order to conduct yourself appropriately in a brother-sister relationship. You may still have a question or two, however.

I challenge you to consider whether you really need an answer to your questions or whether they arise from a simple fear of the unknown.

When a friend gives driving directions through unfamiliar territory, you don't ask for a road map that indicates every pothole, crosswalk, stop sign, and gas station you'll encounter. You ask for a map that gives you a general idea of how to get where you're going. You figure you can negotiate the potholes, crosswalks, stop signs, and the like that confront you on the way.

Similarly here. I believe I have given a clear "way" of where you need to go. You should be able to negotiate the smaller curves and potholes that are likely to come your way. When you see a relational flashing yellow light, when you find yourself in unfamiliar territory, it doesn't mean you have to stop. It simply means slow down!

Follow the rules of prudent driving. Slow down. Look both ways. Try to evaluate the potential dangers. And then proceed with caution.

I haven't had all the experiences a person might have. I haven't met all my brothers and sisters. But I've discovered a few good "rules of the road" that can help you get where you're going safely, pleasurably, and with the greatest blessing to you and your brothers and sisters.

Yes, brother-sister relationships are difficult. They take work. They are not for people who want to take life easy, who never want to think, who want to do nothing except what "everyone else" does.

But God hasn't called us to do what everyone else does. He's called us to be different. He has said that the way leading to life is narrow and only a few find it. The road that leads to destruction is broad, and many people follow it (see Matthew 7:14). God has called us to be perfect even as He is perfect (see Matthew

5:48). He wants us to be alert (see 1 Peter 5:8), to be mentally, emotionally, and spiritually armed for battle (see Ephesians 6:10–18 and 1 Timothy 6:11–14). Brother-sister relationships require mental, emotional, and spiritual preparedness and alertness.

The primary question you need to answer is not whether brother-sister relationships are practical, easy, or avoid all dangers. The primary question you need to answer is whether or not you will be obedient to what God tells you to do.

Is God telling you to walk with integrity before your brothers and sisters? Will brother-sister relationships as described in this book enable you to walk with integrity? Will they help you to bless others? Are you able to walk with integrity and bless others as freely if you allow yourself to be someone's boyfriend, girlfriend, or "serious" dating partner?

You know my answers to these questions. What are yours?

APPENDIXES

APPENDIX A

Brothers and Sisters in Christ: What the Bible Says

The New International Version translates 1 Timothy 5:1 and 2: "Do not rebuke an older man harshly, but exhort him as if he were your father. *Treat younger men as brothers, older women as mothers, and younger women as sisters,* with absolute purity" (emphasis added).

The Revised Standard Version translation is almost identical: "Do not rebuke an older man but exhort him as you would a father; *treat younger men like brothers, older women like mothers, younger women like sisters,* in all purity" (emphasis added).

Many people—indeed, for many years, I myself—have used these verses as the basis for believing in the ideas presented in the pages of this book. "'Treat younger men as brothers . . . and younger women as sisters.' That's what the Bible says. What could be clearer than that?"

There is a problem with that thinking. In the original Greek one finds there is no verb *to treat* in 1 Timothy 5:1 and 2. Instead of a general command to be applied by all believers in all situations, Paul is speaking to Timothy in his role as pastor. Further, Paul is not speaking about how Pastor Timothy should carry out his pastoral duties *in general*; he is telling Timothy how he should communicate with the people under his care *when they have gone astray.* Finally, Paul does not tell Timothy to *treat* these people as brothers and sisters; he tells Timothy to *speak* to them as brothers and sisters ("do not *rebuke,* rather *exhort*").

The New American Standard Version translates well at this point. "Do not sharply rebuke an older man, but rather appeal to him as a father, to the younger men as brothers, the older women as mothers, and the younger women as sisters, in all purity."

Interpreting 1 Timothy 5:1 and 2, then, in its narrowest possible sense, we find that God has made no specific command to "treat younger men as brothers and younger women as sisters" at all times.

But while 1 Timothy 5 gives no specific command to the effect that we are to treat all younger men and women as brothers and sisters, and while there is no other verse that teaches that exact principle with those very words, there can be no doubt that the principle is valid.

In Romans 4:16, we are taught that Abraham is the spiritual father of all believers. According to Hebrews 2:11, 12 and 17, Jesus is our older brother. Romans 8:15 and Galatians 4:6 both teach that all believers have been given a common Spirit by which we cry out to God: "Abba, Father." Further, all believers are heirs to the same birthright (see Romans 8:17; Galatians 3:29; 1 Peter 3:7, for example). There can be little doubt concerning the import of these passages: we are all related. All believers in Christ are related as sons and daughters of God, joint heirs with Christ of the blessings Jesus bought through His life, death, and resurrection. Put another way: we are brothers and sisters *in Christ.*

But we do not even have to rely on this construction. The use of *brothers* especially (though *sisters,* too) is common throughout the New Testament to refer to believers who are unrelated by birth. Acts 6:2 and 3 is one minor example. The twelve apostles "gathered all the disciples together and said, 'Brothers, choose seven men from among you. . . .'" They were referring to the whole group of believers.

In Romans 1:13, Paul addresses the Roman believers as brothers.

In Matthew 5:22–24, Jesus uses the word *brother* to teach relational principles that hold far beyond the bounds of relations between natural-born brothers and sisters.

> Anyone who is angry with his *brother* will be subject to judgment. Again, anyone who says to his *brother*, "Raca," is answerable to the Sanhedrin. . . . Therefore, if you are offering your gift at the altar and there remember that your *brother* has something against you, leave your gift there in front of the altar. First go and be reconciled to your *brother*; then come and offer your gift. (emphasis added)

In James 2:15, James speaks similarly: "Suppose a *brother* or *sister* is without clothes and daily food . . ." (emphasis added). The very fact that he leaves the words *brother* and *sister* indefinite—"*a* brother or sister"—gives additional evidence that James is not speaking merely of brothers and sisters in the flesh. He's referring to believers.

But not only are there theological grounds for speaking of one another as brothers and sisters, and not only are there Scriptural examples of believers speaking of each other in these terms, in at least four passages—Romans 12:10, 1 Thessalonians 4:9–10, Hebrews 13:1, and 2 Peter 1:7)—believers are taught to care for each other with "brotherly love" or "brotherly kindness" (*philadelphia*). In other words, Christians' actions toward one another must be tempered with the kind of love—*brotherly* love, *philadelphia*—that brothers and sisters should have for one another. Brothers and sisters in Christ should treat each other the way brothers and sisters in the flesh are supposed to treat each other. (See chapter 2.)

APPENDIX B

Brother-Sister, Boyfriend-Girlfriend, "Serious" Dating and Marriage Relationships

As you can see from the following charts, I believe boyfriend-girlfriend and "serious" relationships fail to meet many of the requirements God has established for honorable relationships among His people. For that reason, I am convinced no Christian should allow him- or herself to become involved in such relationships. Scripturally, there is no room for relationships based on unspoken, unwanted, unmeant, unintentional vows. There is no room for exclusive ownership relationships in which there is no adequate compensation for the privileges. There is no room outside of marriage for relationships that include sexual intimacy. God grants us none of those rights.

Moreover, God calls us to relationships in which we seek more to bless than to be blessed, more to give than to receive. God calls us to relationships in which honesty and integrity reign supreme. Brothers and sisters pursue these goals with abandon. Whatever will increase the blessing for their brothers and sisters, brothers and sisters pursue it.

If you have a relationship that has all the characteristics of a brother-sister relationship but you prefer to speak of your friend as your boyfriend or girlfriend, I have no quarrel with you. I have no doubt God will look kindly upon you and the way you and your brother or sister are treating each other. I would caution you, however, that your terminology may hinder more than it helps. I have found that for most people, the words *boyfriend* and *girlfriend* tend to connote the kinds of relationship I've described. They may disagree on one or two points: "Well, it doesn't *have* to include physical-sexual intimacy—at least not at the start." But they know what I mean and feel comfortable with my use of the terms. On the other hand, to speak of a brother-sister relationship as boyfriend-girlfriend seems to confuse the issue.

One more comment: I have known plenty of people who speak of themselves as being involved in brother-sister relationships when in fact they treated each other no differently than boyfriends and girlfriends. Oh, they may have denied that they owned each other or demanded exclusivity. Maybe they even avoided sexual intimacy. But the fact was, they treated each other with such exceptional concern compared with the rest of their friends, no one doubted that they were a pair; no one would have dared approach either one for a date. "Brother-sister" in these circumstances was nothing more than a "spiritual" way of saying boyfriend-girlfriend.

As I noted in chapter 3, brothers and sisters use no guile, even against themselves.

Common Characteristics	Type of Relationship			
	Brother-Sister	Boyfriend-Girlfriend	"Serious" Dating	Engagement/ Marriage
Physical-social intimacy	✓	✓	✓	✓
Physical-emotional intimacy	✓	✓	✓	✓
Growing knowledge, affection, and trust (i.e., growing friendship)	✓	✓	✓	✓
Based on vows or promises that are:				
Desired			✓	✓
Meant as stated				✓
Participants:				
Are thinking of marrying each other			✓	
Are ready, willing, and able to fulfill marriage vows to one another				✓
Have a conscious sense that their relationship is filled with integrity	✓		✓	✓
Speak the truth in love at all times	✓	✓	✓	✓
Confuse romantic attraction, commitment, and obligation		✓	✓	?
Speak to one another with guile		✓	not as often as in B-G relationships	?
Enter relationship for selfish reasons		✓	✓	?

Table 1: *Common* Characteristics of Various Male-Female Relationships

Table 2: Essential Characteristics of Various Male-Female Relationships				
Essential Characteristics	**Type of Relationship**			
	Brother-Sister	Boyfriend-Girlfriend	"Serious" Dating	Engagement/Marriage
Based on mutual allegiance to the Lord	✓			
Based on mutual vows or promises		✓	✓	✓
Mutual vows or promises are:				
Spoken			✓	✓
Communicated intentionally			✓	✓
Thoroughly defined				✓
"Until I decide not to fulfill them anymore"		✓		
"Until *we* decide not to fulfill them anymore"			✓	
"Till death do us part"				✓
Sense of ownership/obligation		✓	✓	✓
Exclusive (unique—only one such relationship at a time; interaction with others is limited)		✓	✓	✓
Sexual intimacy		✓	✓	✓
Participants:				
Show equal concern to "outsiders" as to one another	✓ (See chapter 2)			
Enjoy unlimited social interaction with one another and "outsiders"	✓ (See chapter 9)			
Speak the truth in love at all times	✓ (See chapter 3)			
When they make vows or promises: intend them, want them, mean them, speak them, fulfill them	✓ (See chapter 4)			

Table 2 continued: Essential Characteristics of Various Male-Female Relationships				
Esential Characteristics	**Type of Relationship**			
	Brother-Sister	**Boyfriend-Girlfriend**	**"Serious" Dating**	**Engagement/Marriage**
Participants:				
Distinguish between romantic attraction, commitment, and obligation	✓ (See chapter 5)			
Guard their hearts	✓ (See chapter 5)			
Avoid ownership obligations	✓ (See chapter 6)			
Avoid sexual intimacy	✓ (See chapter 7)			
Pursue God's desire for them to bless others	✓ (See chapter 1)			
Trust the Lord to fulfill their hearts' desire	✓ (See chapter 8)			

APPENDIX C

How Relationships Progress Toward Marriage

I believe the following diagram accurately and adequately describes the progression of a male-female relationship from acquaintanceship to marriage following current social norms in the United States:

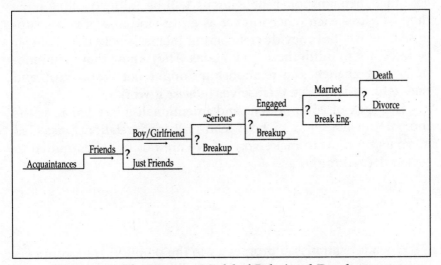

Diagram 1:. The Western Model of Relational Development

In this scenario, a guy and girl become boyfriend and girlfriend at the moment they imply to each other that they have some kind of commitment to one another. This implication is communicated when one or the other of the two participants begins to take advantage of or begins to demand one of the essential characteristics or defining rights of marriage: physical-sexual intimacy, ownership, or exclusiveness (see Table 2 in Appendix B). A couple may become boyfriend and girlfriend without ever having established a friendship relationship. That's why *Friends* is placed in parentheses.

Talley and Reed are correct (see question 11 at the end of chapter 9): a man and woman *can* be "more than friends," without ever having become friends. As soon as a couple engages in the implied commitments of a boyfriend-girlfriend relationship, as one young woman said, "A direction has been set. You're going to get married unless you break up." That's the reason for the one-way arrows. You can move from being Boyfriend and Girlfriend to being "Serious," but not the other way around. If a couple doesn't move on to the next stage in the relationship (being "Serious"), then they will eventually break up.

In boyfriend-girlfriend relationships, the participants usually *hope* that their unspoken obligations will be fulfilled—they hope they will love each other forever as a husband and wife are supposed to love. But they do not commit themselves to do whatever is necessary to fulfill those obligations. They know that their emotions may change, the relationship "might not work out," and they refuse to obligate themselves to *make* it work.

This lack of commitment and intentionality is what is at the root of my objection to boyfriend-girlfriend relationships: God gives us no right to make vows if we are not fully committed to seeing them through.

                                          ❧ ❧ ❧

When a relationship progresses to the point where a couple is thinking more seriously about the possibility of marriage, the participants will often enter into what they call a "serious" relationship. At this point they verbally and explicitly commit themselves to go out with no one else, to "pursue the possibility of marriage," etc. So-called "serious" relationships are rarely defined with any degree of precision (see chapter 4). Participants still refuse to commit themselves to marry each other. In chapters 4 and 6, I explain in some detail what my objections are to these kinds of commitments.

ᔥ ᔥ ᔥ

Eventually, some couples become engaged. When a couple becomes engaged, they verbally and explicitly tell each other that they intend to marry. Despite these clear promises to marry, many couples view engagement as a time for finally determining whether or not they should marry. To quote Small:

> Engagement is regarded today as the final factor in wise marriage choice. It is a period of courtship, the objective of which is settled and the consummation of which is now in view. It is a time during which the couple can make a careful check to see if they are well prepared to enter into the uncertainties of marriage with a well-based confidence and plan. . . .
>
> Engagement serves as an appropriate transition from the relative irresponsibility of single status to the responsible commitments of marriage. It is a time of specific planning and testing. Attention so largely focused previously on personality and background factors . . . now focuses upon whether that relationship has adequate resources to weather the problems of marriage. Four principles gain major consideration: adaptability, communication, adjustment to reality, and the problem-solving and decision-making abilities.[1]

I object to this perspective of engagement because God gives His children no right to make promises they are not sure they want or are able to fulfill. No one needs to enter an engaged relationship in order to "plan" and "test" or to consider their ability to "adapt," "communicate," "adjust to reality," "solve problems," or "make decisions"! A close brother-sister relationship is perfectly adequate for all these endeavors.

ॐ ॐ ॐ

Finally, when a couple gets married, they make vows at the wedding that they think they mean to fulfill. However, the divorce rate today in the United States is close to 50 percent, and evangelical Christians have a divorce rate only a few points lower than that. Obviously, someone (or two) in each of these couples is failing to fulfill the vows of marriage! Is it possible that the lack of emphasis on integrity at earlier stages in these relationships leads to the lack of integrity in marriage? I believe this quite probable.

In opposition to this culturally accepted model, I propose the following:

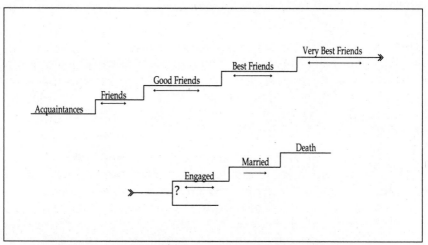

Diagram 2: Brother-Sister Model of Relational Development

Some people ask, "Where does the brother-sister relationship come in?" The answer is: the entire diagram describes a brother-sister relationship. Children of God are no more or less brothers and sisters when they are married than when they are mutual unknowns. As we point out in Table 2 of Appendix B, brother-sister relationships are based on mutual allegiance to the Lord—not any other thing.

But now for a description of Diagram 2, previous page. Instead of all the decision points, question marks, and unnecessary and illegitimate commitments on the way toward marriage, I believe there should be one major point of transition, one time and place at which you answer all your questions, take your oath, and make your vows. I believe the point at which all these things should occur is engagement or, perhaps more appropriately, betrothal.

To be *betrothed* means to be promised. People used to speak of "plighting" (pledging, promising) one's "troth." *Troth* means faithfulness, loyalty, promise. But whether we call it engagement or betrothal, the main thing people need to attend to is that their promises are true and they will do whatever they must in order to fulfill them.

At the point of engagement or betrothal the great transition should occur. It is here that one should make one's vows and plan to keep them. Before one makes a vow, all one's questions should be answered concerning whether or not he or she intends to fulfill it. It is at the point of engagement that the big shift should occur between being "mere" friends to being committed to one another as husband and wife for the rest of our lives.

At betrothal a couple is not yet married, but they are on their way toward marriage and they should exert every effort to ensure that they get there, unless God intervenes and allows one of them to die.

In the brother-sister model, there are smooth transitions from acquaintanceship to friendship to good friendship to best friendship . . . or vice versa. As indicated by the double-pointed arrows, one can move just as easily up or down the scale of intimacy within this sphere. It is only at the point of engagement that a major hurdle must be crossed as a couple considers whether or not they will commit themselves to one another for the rest of their lives. Once they have made that commitment, the direction has been set, and their relationship progresses rather smoothly to the point of marriage and beyond.

Though the wedding itself marks a significant transition point—it is the point at which a couple becomes legally, socially, and familially recognized as being given to each other (prior to that point they are only promised)—that the wedding itself will occur or that the man and woman will be present for the wedding should never be open to question.

Instead of following the culturally accepted pattern of making vows that have an ever-increasing probability of fulfillment, brothers and sisters make one vow at one time that *will* be fulfilled. Period. "So help me God."

NOTES

Chapter 1—What Do You Have in Mind?

1. "Person to Person," *Campus Life* (March 1985): 17.

Chapter 3—Speaking the Truth in Love

1. David Augsburger, *Caring Enough to Confront* (Regal Books, 1981), 10, 25.

2. Ibid., 20.

Chapter 4—"Under the Terms of This Contract . . ."

1. Mark L. Knapp, *Nonverbal Communication in Human Interaction* (Holt, Rinehart and Winston, 1972), 12.

2. Lionel Haines, "Shattered Dreams: 'I Was Told to Get Out and Never Come Back,'" *Success* (June 1989): 46.

3. Reed, Bobbie and Jim Talley, *Too Close, Too Soon* (Nashville,TN: Thomas Nelson Publishers, 1982), 42ff.

4. Ibid., 50–51.

Chapter 7—Sex

1. Gary Smalley and John Trent, *The Blessing* (Nashville, TN: Thomas Nelson Publishers, 1986), 42.

2. *Leadership*:9 (Winter 1988):108–112.

3. "Private Sins of Public Ministry," *Leadership*:9 (Winter 1988): 19.

4. Dwight Hervey Small, *Design for Christian Marriage* (Spire Books, 1971), 188.

5. Ken Wilson, "Marriage Preparation: Early Enough to Make a Difference," *Pastoral Renewal* (September 1985): 29.

6. "Counseling the Seductive Female," *Leadership*:9 [Winter 1988]: 54.

7. Ibid.

8. Joyce Huggett, *Dating, Sex & Friendship* (InterVarsity Press, 1985), 99.

9. Ibid., 96.

10. Ibid., 98.

11. Quoted in *Focus on the Family Magazine* (February 1989): 5.

12. *The Interpreter's Dictionary of the Bible*, Vol. 2 (Abingdon Press, 1962), 321.

13. Wilson, "Marriage Preparation," *Pastoral Renewal*, 29.

14. *Small, Design for Christian Marriage*, 195 (emphasis added).

15. Ibid., 195–196.

16. Burdette Palmberg, "Private Sins of Public Ministry," *Leadership*, 20.

Chapter 8—Day Time, Night Time, Lots of Time

1. Jim Talley and Bobbie Reed, *Too Close Too Soon* (Thomas Nelson Publishers, 1982), 30.

2. Ibid., 41.

3. Ibid.

4. Ibid., 30-34.

5. Ibid., 40.

6. Ibid.

Chapter 9—No Grievous Burden

1. Ernst Lange, *Ten Great Freedoms* (InterVarsity Press, 1970).

2. Dick Purnell, *Beating the Break-Up Habit* (San Bernardino, CA: Here's Life Publishers, Inc., 1984).

Chapter 10—How Do Brothers and Sisters Date?

1. *Campus Life* (November 1985): 35.

Appendix C—How Relationships Progress Toward Marriage

1. Small, *Design for Christian Marriage* , 232.

ABOUT THE AUTHOR

A former assistant pastor and long-time counselor to young adults, John Holzmann earned the M.Div. from Westminster Theological Seminary, Philadelphia. For the past six years he has been involved in publishing for Christian missions. He has authored over seventy articles and edited three books including Don Hamilton's *Tentmakers Speak* (Gospel Light/Regal Books). He is married and the father of four children.

Palatino type—best known as a contemporary *italic* typeface—was a post-World War II design crafted by the talented young German calligrapher Hermann Zapf. For inspiration, Zapf drew upon the writing legacy of a group of Italian Renaissance writing masters, in which the typeface's namesake Giovanni Battista Palatino was numbered. Giovanni Palatino's *Libro nuovo d'imparare a scrivera* was published in Rome in 1540 and became one of the most used, wide-ranging writing manuals of the sixteenth century. Zapf was an apt student of the European Masters, and contemporary Palatino is his contribution to modern typography.

Substantive Editing:
Michael S. Hyatt

Copy Editing:
Susan Kirby

Cover Design:
Steve Diggs & Friends
Nashville, Tennessee

Page Composition:
Xerox Ventura Publisher
Printware 720 IQ Laser Printer

Printing and Binding:
Maple-Vail Book Manufacturing Group
York, Pennsylvania

Cover Printing:
Strine Printing
York, Pennsylvania